THE AUSTRALIAN
Women's Weekly
home cooked

CW01019838

THE AUSTRALIAN
Women's Weekly

Contents

Cooking for yourself, your family and your friends need not be difficult – get some good ingredients, give yourself the time to get it all ready and the results will be admired and devoured by all! The simplest way to ensure you get a good meal is to buy the ingredients, prepare them yourself and serve them the way you prefer. There is always time to be good to yourself, so nurture your future health with some great home cooking.

Pamela Clark

Hearty Breakfast

TRADITIONAL
porridge

SUNDAY FRY-UP

Fruity muesli

HOT MUFFINS
straight from the oven

AND ALL THE OTHER PERFECT
INGREDIENTS FOR A GOOD
START TO THE DAY

Traditional porridge

3½ cups (875ml) hot water
1½ cups (135g) rolled oats
½ cup (125ml) milk
2 tablespoons caster sugar
1 teaspoon ground cinnamon

1 Combine the water and oats in medium saucepan over medium heat; cook, stirring, about 5 minutes or until porridge is thick and creamy.
2 Stir in milk. Serve sprinkled with combined sugar and cinnamon.

prep and cook time 10 minutes
serves 4
nutritional count per serving 4.1g total fat (1.3g saturated fat); 782kJ (187 cal); 31.4g carbohydrate; 4.7g protein; 2.4g fibre

Rice porridge with raisins

½ cup (100g) gluten-free rice
½ cup (125ml) water
2 cups (500ml) skimmed milk
1 tablespoon brown sugar
¼ cup (40g) raisins
pinch nutmeg
⅔ cup (160ml) skimmed milk, warmed, extra

1 Combine rice and the water in small saucepan; bring to a boil. Reduce heat; simmer, uncovered, until liquid is absorbed.
2 Add milk, sugar and raisins; simmer about 20 minutes or until rice is tender, stirring occasionally. Stir in nutmeg; serve warm with extra milk.

prep and cook time 40 minutes
serves 4
nutritional count per serving 0.4g total fat (0.2g saturated fat); 789kJ (188 cal); 38.6g carbohydrate; 0.7g fibre

Bircher muesli

2 cups (180g) rolled oats
1¼ cups (310ml) apple juice
1 cup (280g) natural yogurt
2 medium green-skinned apples (300g)
¼ cup (35g) roasted slivered almonds
¼ cup (40g) currants
¼ cup (20g) toasted shredded coconut
1 teaspoon ground cinnamon
½ cup (140g) natural yogurt, extra

1 Combine oats, juice and yogurt in medium bowl. Cover; refrigerate overnight.
2 Peel, core and coarsely grate one apple; stir into oat mixture with nuts, currants, coconut and cinnamon.
3 Core and thinly slice remaining apple. Serve muesli topped with extra yogurt and apple slices.

prep time 10 minutes (plus refrigeration)
serves 6
nutritional count per serving 9.2g total fat (3g saturated fat); 1120kJ (268 cal); 36.1g carbohydrate; 8.1g protein; 3.9g fibre

Roasted muesli with fruit & honey

2 cups (180g) rolled oats
1 cup (110g) rolled rice
¼ cup (15g) unprocessed wheat bran
¼ cup (50g) pepitas
1 teaspoon ground cinnamon
⅓ cup (115g) honey
1 tablespoon vegetable oil
¾ cup (35g) flaked coconut
⅓ cup (50g) coarsely chopped dried apricots
⅓ cup (20g) coarsely chopped dried apples
⅓ cup (55g) sultanas
¼ cup (35g) dried cranberries, chopped coarsely

1 Preheat oven to 180°C/160°C fan-assisted.
2 Combine oats and rice in large bowl, then spread evenly between two oven trays. Roast, uncovered, in oven 5 minutes.
3 Stir bran, pepitas and cinnamon into oat mixtures, then drizzle evenly with combined honey and oil; stir to combine. Roast, uncovered, 5 minutes. Stir in coconut. Roast, uncovered, further 5 minutes.
4 Remove trays from oven; place muesli mixture in same large bowl, stir in remaining ingredients. Serve with milk or yogurt.

prep and cook time 30 minutes
serves 6
nutritional count
per serving 16.1g total fat (4.8g saturated); 1768kJ (423 cal); 52.8g carbohydrate; 7.3g protein; 11.1g fibre

YOU CAN STORE THIS ROASTED MUESLI IN AN AIRTIGHT CONTAINER, IN A COOL PLACE, FOR UP TO TWO WEEKS.

French toast

3 eggs, beaten lightly
⅓ cup (80ml) double cream
⅓ cup (80ml) milk
¼ teaspoon ground cinnamon
1 tablespoon caster sugar
12 x 2cm slices french bread stick
50g butter

1 Combine egg, cream, milk, cinnamon and sugar in large bowl. Dip bread slices into egg mixture.

2 Melt half of the butter in large frying pan; cook half of the bread slices until browned both sides. Repeat with remaining butter and bread.

3 Serve french toast sprinkled with sifted icing sugar, if desired.

prep and cook time 15 minutes
serves 4
nutritional count per serving 24.8g total fat (14.3g saturated fat); 1450kJ (347 cal); 22.2g carbohydrate; 8.8g protein; 1.1g fibre

Pancakes with lemon & sugar

2 cups (300g) plain flour
4 eggs, beaten lightly
2 cups (500ml) milk, approximately
40g butter
¼ cup (60ml) lemon juice, approximately
2 tablespoons sugar, approximately

1 Place flour in medium bowl. Make well in centre; gradually whisk or stir in egg and enough of the milk to make a thin, smooth batter.
2 Heat large frying pan over high heat a few minutes. Place ½ teaspoon butter in pan; swirl around pan until greased all over. Pour ¼ cup of the batter from jug into centre of pan; quickly tilt pan so that batter runs from centre around edge.
3 When pancake is browned lightly underneath, turn and brown other side. This can be done using spatula or egg slide, or pancake can be tossed and flipped over back into the pan; this takes a little practice.
4 Serve pancakes, as they are made, on warm plates; spread one side with a little of the butter. Drizzle with juice; sprinkle with sugar.

prep and cook time 25 minutes
serves 4
nutritional count per pancake 19.3g total fat (10.4g saturated fat); 2245kJ (537 cal); 69.7g carbohydrate; 19.2g protein; 2.9g fibre

Egg in toast

4 thick slices white bread
25g butter
4 eggs
2 tablespoons tomato chutney

1 Cut a 7cm circle from the centre of each slice of bread. Discard centre pieces.
2 Melt butter in large frying pan; cook bread until browned lightly on one side. Turn; crack one egg into the centre of each piece of bread.
3 Cook, over low heat, until egg white just sets. Using spatula, gently lift toast onto serving plates. Serve with chutney.

prep and cook time 15 minutes
serves 4
nutritional count per serving 11.5g total fat (5.1g saturated fat); 1007kJ (241 cal); 23.5g carbohydrate; 10.1g protein; 1.4g fibre

Ham & cheese toastie with fried egg

8 slices wholemeal bread (360g)
8 slices ham (240g)
40g butter
4 eggs
cheese béchamel
20g butter
1 tablespoon plain flour
¾ cup (180ml) milk
½ cup (60g) finely grated cheddar cheese
1 tablespoon finely chopped fresh flat-leaf parsley

1 Make cheese béchamel.
2 Spread béchamel onto bread slices. Top four slices with ham then remaining bread.
3 Melt butter in large frying pan. Add sandwiches; toast, in batches, until browned both sides.
4 Fry eggs in same pan until cooked; place an egg on each sandwich.
cheese béchamel Melt butter in small saucepan, add flour; cook, stirring, until mixture bubbles and thickens. Gradually add milk; cook, stirring, until sauce boils and thickens. Remove from heat; stir in cheese and parsley.

prep and cook time 35 minutes
serves 4
nutritional count per serving 29.2g total fat (15.2g saturated fat); 2328kJ (557 cal); 38.6g carbohydrate; 32.3g protein; 5.8g fibre

Courgette & mushroom omelette

IT'S IMPORTANT TO WORK QUICKLY WHEN MAKING AN OMELETTE OR THE EGG MIXTURE IN CONTACT WITH THE PAN WILL COOK TOO MUCH AND WILL BROWN AND TOUGHEN; THE FINISHED OMELETTE SHOULD BE ONLY BROWNED LIGHTLY UNDERNEATH.

10g butter
1 clove garlic, crushed
25g button mushrooms, sliced thinly
¼ cup (50g) coarsely grated courgette
1 spring onion, chopped finely
2 eggs
1 tablespoon water
¼ cup (30g) coarsely grated cheddar cheese

1 Heat half of the butter in small frying pan; cook garlic and mushroom, stirring, over medium heat about 2 minutes or until mushroom is lightly browned. Add courgette and onion; cook, stirring, about 1 minute or until courgette begins to soften. Remove vegetable mixture from pan; cover to keep warm.
2 Beat eggs and the water in small bowl. Add cheese; whisk until combined.

3 Heat remaining butter in same pan; swirl pan so butter covers base. Pour egg mixture into pan; cook, tilting pan, over medium heat until almost set.
4 Place vegetable mixture evenly over half of the omelette; using spatula, flip other half over vegetable mixture. Using spatula, slide omelette gently onto serving plate.

prep and cook time 20 minutes
serves 1
nutritional count per serving 11.7g total fat (6.1g saturated fat); 606kJ (145 cal); 0.8g carbohydrate; 8.9g protein; 0.9g fibre

Sautéed mushrooms

50g butter, chopped
1 small brown onion (80g), chopped finely
500g button mushrooms, halved
1 tablespoon malt vinegar
⅓ cup coarsely chopped fresh chives

1 Melt butter in large frying pan; cook onion, stirring, until soft.
2 Add mushrooms; cook, stirring occasionally, 10 minutes or until mushrooms are tender. Add vinegar; bring to the boil. Remove from heat; stir in chives.
3 Serve mushrooms on thick toast, if desired.

prep and cook time 30 minutes
serves 4
nutritional count per serving 10.7g total fat (6.8g saturated fat); 531kJ (127 cal); 1.7g carbohydrate; 4.9g protein; 3.5g fibre

Sunday fry-up

50g butter
300g button mushrooms, sliced thickly
8 chipolata sausages (240g)
4 rashers bacon (280g)
1 tablespoon olive oil
2 medium tomatoes (190g), halved
4 eggs

1 Melt butter in medium saucepan; cook mushrooms, stirring, for 5 minutes or until tender.
2 Meanwhile, cook sausages and bacon in heated oiled large frying pan until bacon is crisp and sausages are cooked through. Remove from pan; cover to keep warm. Drain fat from pan.
3 Preheat grill. Place tomato halves, cut-side up, onto baking tray. Cook under grill until browned lightly and tender.
4 Meanwhile, heat oil in same uncleaned frying pan. Break eggs into pan; cook until egg white has set and yolk is cooked as desired.
5 Serve mushrooms, sausages, bacon, tomato and eggs with thick toast, if desired.

prep and cook time 30 minutes
serves 4
nutritional count per serving 41.3g total fat (16.9g saturated fat); 2203kJ (527 cal); 4.4g carbohydrate; 34g protein; 3.2g fibre

Scrambled eggs

250g cherry tomatoes
1 tablespoon olive oil
8 slices thin bacon (240g)
8 eggs
½ cup (125ml) double cream
2 tablespoons finely chopped fresh chives
30g butter
4 slices crusty bread, toasted

1 Preheat grill. Toss tomatoes in oil. Grill bacon and tomato until bacon is crisp and tomato skins start to split. Cover to keep warm.
2 Meanwhile, combine eggs, cream and chives in medium bowl; beat lightly with fork.
3 Heat butter in large frying pan over medium heat. Add egg mixture, wait a few seconds, then use a wide spatula to gently scrape the set egg mixture along the base of the pan; cook until creamy and just set.
4 Serve toast topped with egg, bacon and tomatoes.

prep and cook time 25 minutes
serves 4
nutritional count per serving 52g total fat (23.9g saturated fat); 3223kJ (771 cal); 40g carbohydrate; 37.6g protein; 2.5g fibre

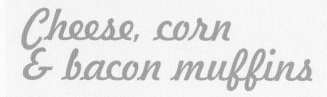

Cheese, corn & bacon muffins

½ cup (85g) polenta
½ cup (125ml) milk
3 bacon rashers (210g), rind removed, chopped finely
4 spring onions, chopped finely
1½ cups (225g) self-raising flour
1 tablespoon caster sugar
310g can corn kernels, drained
125g can creamed corn
100g butter, melted
2 eggs, beaten lightly
50g piece cheddar cheese
¼ cup (30g) coarsely grated cheddar cheese

1 Preheat oven to 180°C/160°C fan-assisted. Oil 12-hole (⅓ cup/80ml) muffin tin.

2 Mix polenta and milk in small bowl, cover; stand 20 minutes.

3 Meanwhile, cook bacon, stirring, in heated small frying pan for 2 minutes. Add onion to pan; cook, stirring, for another 2 minutes. Remove pan from heat; cool 5 minutes.

4 Sift flour and sugar into large bowl; stir in corn kernels, creamed corn and bacon mixture. Add melted butter, eggs and polenta mixture; mix muffin batter only until just combined.

5 Spoon 1 tablespoon of the batter into each hole of muffin tin. Cut piece of cheese into 12 equal pieces; place one piece in the centre of each muffin tin hole. Divide remaining batter among tin holes; sprinkle grated cheese over each.

6 Bake muffins about 20 minutes. Turn onto wire rack. Serve muffins warm.

prep and cook time 45 minutes (plus standing time)
makes 12
nutritional count per muffin 12.5g total fat (7.1g saturated fat); 1087kJ (260 cal); 25.7g carbohydrate; 10g protein; 1.9g fibre

Banana & cinnamon muffins

2 cups (300g) self-raising flour
⅓ cup (50g) plain flour
1 teaspoon ground cinnamon
½ teaspoon bicarbonate of soda
½ cup (110g) firmly packed brown sugar
1 cup mashed banana
2 eggs
¾ cup (180ml) buttermilk
⅓ cup (80ml) vegetable oil
½ teaspoon ground cinnamon, extra
cream cheese topping
125g cream cheese, softened
¼ cup (40g) icing sugar

1 Preheat oven to 200°C/180°C fan-assisted. Grease 12-hole (⅓-cup/80ml) muffin tin.
2 Sift flours, cinnamon, soda and sugar into large bowl; stir in banana then combined eggs, buttermilk and oil. Divide mixture among muffin tin holes.
3 Bake muffins about 20 minutes. Stand in tin 5 minutes; turn onto wire rack to cool.
4 Make cream cheese topping.
5 Spread cold muffins with topping; sprinkle with extra cinnamon.
cream cheese topping Beat ingredients in small bowl with electric mixer until smooth.

prep and cook time 40 minutes
makes 12
nutritional count per muffin 10.3g total fat (3.2g saturated fat); 1133kJ (271 cal); 37.9g carbohydrate; 5.8g protein; 1.5g fibre

Overnight date & muesli muffins

1¼ cups (185g) plain flour
1¼ cups (160g) toasted muesli
1 teaspoon ground cinnamon
1 teaspoon bicarbonate of soda
½ cup (110g) firmly packed brown sugar
½ cup (30g) unprocessed bran
¾ cup (120g) coarsely chopped pitted dates
1½ cups (375ml) buttermilk
½ cup (125ml) vegetable oil
1 egg, beaten lightly

1   Combine ingredients in large bowl, stir until just combined. Cover; refrigerate overnight.
2   Preheat oven to 180°C/160°C fan-assisted. Grease 12-hole (⅓-cup/80ml) muffin tin. Divide mixture among muffin tin holes.
3   Bake muffins about 20 minutes. Stand in tin 5 minutes; turn, top-side up, onto wire rack to cool.

prep and cook time 30 minutes (plus refrigeration)
makes 12
nutritional count per muffin 11.9g total fat (2.1g saturated fat); 1204kJ (288 cal); 38g carbohydrate; 5.4g protein; 3.7g fibre

Berry buttermilk muffins

2½ cups (375g) self-raising flour
90g chilled butter, chopped
1 cup (220g) caster sugar
1¼ cups (310ml) buttermilk
1 egg, beaten lightly
200g fresh or frozen mixed berries

1   Preheat oven to 180°C/160°C fan-assisted. Grease 12-hole (⅓-cup/80ml) muffin tin.
2   Sift flour into large bowl; rub in butter. Stir in sugar, buttermilk and egg. Do not over-mix; mixture should be lumpy. Add berries; stir through gently. Spoon mixture into muffin tin holes.
3   Bake muffins about 20 minutes. Stand in tin 5 minutes; turn, top-side up, onto wire rack to cool.

prep and cook time 30 minutes
makes 12
nutritional count per muffin 7.5g total fat (4.6g saturated fat); 1095kJ (262 cal); 42.4g carbohydrate; 5.1g protein; 1.6g fibre

Mid-morning Cuppa

Melting moments

WARM PIKELETS
dripping with butter

CRUMBLY SCOTTISH
shortbread

CHOC-CHIP COOKIES

MANY OF LIFE'S BIG QUESTIONS
HAVE BEEN RESOLVED OVER
A MID-MORNING CUPPA AND A
STILL-WARM BISCUIT OR PASTRY

Pikelets

1 cup (150g) self-raising flour
¼ cup (55g) caster sugar
pinch bicarbonate of soda
1 egg, beaten lightly
¾ cup (180g) milk, approximately

1 Sift dry ingredients into medium bowl. Make well in centre; gradually stir in egg and enough milk to give a smooth, pouring consistency.
2 Drop tablespoons of batter into heated oiled large frying pan; allow room for spreading. When bubbles begin to appear, turn pikelets; cook until lightly browned on other side. Serve warm with butter or cream and jam.

prep and cook time 40 minutes
makes 18
nutritional count per pikelet 3.2g total fat (1.5g saturated fat); 882kJ (211 cal); 38.2g carbohydrate; 6.2g protein; 1.3g fibre

Oaty apple pikelets

2 cups (500ml) skimmed milk
1 cup (120g) oat bran
½ cup (75g) plain flour
2 tablespoons brown sugar
½ teaspoon mixed spice
2 eggs
1 large apple (200g), peeled, cored, chopped finely
1 tablespoon lemon juice
½ cup (175g) honey
½ cup (100g) low-fat ricotta cheese

1 Blend or process milk, bran, flour, sugar, spice and eggs until smooth; pour into large jug. Stir in apple and juice, cover; refrigerate 30 minutes (mixture will separate during refrigeration).
2 Heat lightly oiled large frying pan. Stir mixture to combine; using ¼-cup batter for each pikelet (mixture will be runny), cook two pikelets at a time, uncovered, until bubbles appear on the surface. Turn; cook until browned lightly. Remove pikelets from pan; cover to keep warm. Repeat with remaining batter to make 12 pikelets.
3 Divide pikelets among plates; top with honey and ricotta.

prep and cook time 25 minutes (plus refrigeration time)
serves 4
nutritional count per serving 7.3g total fat (2.7g saturated fat); 1973kJ (472 cal); 83.6g carbohydrate; 19g protein; 6.3g fibre

Fruit scrolls with spiced yogurt

40g butter
¼ teaspoon ground nutmeg
1½ tablespoons brown sugar
1 tablespoon ground cinnamon
1 small apple (130g), peeled, cored, grated coarsely
⅓ cup (50g) finely chopped dried apricots
½ cup (125ml) orange juice
1 sheet ready-rolled puff pastry
½ cup (140g) natural yogurt
1 tablespoon honey
icing sugar, for dusting

1 Preheat oven to 200°C/180°C fan-assisted. Lightly grease oven tray.
2 Melt half of the butter in small saucepan; cook nutmeg, sugar and half the cinnamon, stirring, over low heat, until sugar dissolves. Stir in apple, apricot and half the juice; bring to a boil. Reduce heat; simmer, uncovered, 2 minutes. Remove from heat; stir in remaining juice. Cool.
3 Spread fruit mixture over pastry sheet; roll into log. Cut log into quarters; place 5cm apart on tray, brush with remaining melted butter. Bake, uncovered, about 20 minutes or until scrolls are cooked through.
4 Meanwhile, combine yogurt, honey and remaining cinnamon in small bowl.
5 Dust hot scrolls with sifted icing sugar; serve with spiced yogurt.

prep and cook time 35 minutes
serves 4
nutritional count per serving 9.5g total fat (6.2g saturated fat); 786kJ (188 cal); 23.0g carbohydrate; 2.5g protein; 1.6g fibre

Chocolate hazelnut croissants

2 sheets ready-rolled puff pastry
⅓ cup (110g) chocolate hazelnut spread
30g dark chocolate, grated finely
25g butter, melted
1 tablespoon icing sugar

1 Preheat oven to 220°C/200°C fan-assisted. Grease two oven trays.
2 Cut pastry sheets diagonally to make four triangles. Spread chocolate spread over triangles, leaving a 1cm border; sprinkle each evenly with chocolate.
3 Roll triangles, starting at one wide end; place 3cm apart on trays with the tips tucked under and the ends slightly curved in to form crescent shape. Brush croissants with melted butter.
4 Bake croissants about 12 minutes or until browned lightly and cooked through. Serve warm or at room temperature, dusted with icing sugar.

prep and cook time 30 minutes
makes 8
nutritional count per croissant
17.7g total fat (4.8g saturated fat); 1166kJ (279 cal); 26.4g carbohydrate; 3.4g protein; 0.9g fibre

FOR A SAVOURY ALTERNATIVE, REPLACE THE HAZELNUT SPREAD AND CHOCOLATE WITH A MIXED-HERB CREAM CHEESE AND SERVE TOPPED WITH SLICED SMOKED SALMON OR TROUT.

Vanilla currant cookies

125g butter, softened
1 teaspoon vanilla extract
¾ cup (165g) caster sugar
1 egg
2 cups (300g) self-raising flour
½ cup (40g) desiccated coconut
¼ cup (40g) currants
vanilla icing
1½ cups (240g) icing sugar
2 teaspoons vanilla extract
1½ teaspoons butter, softened
1 tablespoon milk, approximately

1　Preheat oven to 200°C/180°C fan-assisted. Grease oven trays.
2　Beat butter, extract, sugar and egg in small bowl with electric mixer until light and fluffy. Transfer mixture to large bowl, stir in sifted flour, coconut and currants.
3　Shape rounded teaspoons of mixture into balls; place onto trays about 5cm apart. Flatten with hand until about 5mm thick.
4　Bake cookies about 10 minutes or until browned lightly. Cool on trays.
5　Spread cookies thinly with vanilla icing, place on wire racks to set.
vanilla icing　Sift icing sugar into medium heatproof bowl, stir in extract and butter, then enough milk to give a thick paste. Stir over hot water until spreadable.

prep and cook time 55 minutes
(plus cooling time)
makes 40
nutritional count per cookie 3.6g total fat (2.4g saturated fat); 414kJ (99 cal); 16.2g carbohydrate; 1g protein; 0.5g fibre

Oatflake cookies

1 cup (90g) rolled oats
1 cup (150g) plain flour
1 cup (220g) firmly packed brown sugar
½ cup (40g) desiccated coconut
125g butter
2 tablespoons golden syrup
1 tablespoon water
½ teaspoon bicarbonate of soda

1 Preheat oven to 160°C/140°C fan-assisted. Grease oven trays; line with baking parchment.
2 Combine oats, sifted flour, sugar and coconut in large bowl.
3 Stir butter, syrup and the water in small saucepan over low heat until smooth; stir in soda. Stir into dry ingredients.
4 Roll level tablespoons of mixture into balls; place about 5cm apart on trays, flatten slightly. Bake about 20 minutes; cool on trays.

prep and cook time 35 minutes
makes 25

nutritional count per cookie 5.4g total fat (3.6g saturated fat); 514kJ (123 cal); 17.2g carbohydrate; 1.2g protein; 0.7g fibre

Choc-chip cookies

125g butter, softened
½ teaspoon vanilla extract
⅓ cup (75g) caster sugar
⅓ cup (75g) firmly packed brown sugar
1 egg
1 cup (150g) plain flour
½ teaspoon bicarbonate of soda
150g milk eating chocolate, chopped coarsely
½ cup (50g) walnuts, chopped coarsely

1 Preheat oven to 180°C/160°C fan-assisted. Grease oven trays; line with baking parchment.

2 Beat butter, extract, sugars and egg in small bowl with electric mixer until smooth; do not overbeat. Transfer mixture to medium bowl; stir in sifted flour and soda then chocolate and nuts.

3 Drop level tablespoons of mixture onto trays 5cm apart. Bake about 15 minutes; cool on trays.

prep and cook time 40 minutes
makes 24
nutritional count per cookie 7.9g total fat (4.7g saturated fat); 564kJ (135 cal); 14.3g carbohydrate; 1.5g protein; 0.7g fibre

THIS RECIPE CALLS FOR COARSELY CHOPPED WALNUTS. TO CHOP THEM, USE A LARGE, HEAVY KNIFE OR PULSE THEM IN A FOOD PROCESSOR: DON'T OVER-PULSE OR THEY'LL TURN TO PASTE.

Almond jam drops

125g butter, softened
½ teaspoon vanilla extract
½ cup (110g) caster sugar
1 cup (120g) ground almonds
1 egg
⅔ cup (100g) plain flour
2 tablespoons raspberry jam

1 Preheat oven to 180°C/160°C fan-assisted. Grease oven trays; line with baking parchment.
2 Beat butter, extract, sugar and ground almonds in small bowl with electric mixer until light and fluffy. Add egg, beating until just combined; stir in sifted flour.
3 Drop level tablespoons of mixture on trays 5cm apart. Use handle of wooden spoon to make small hole (about 1cm deep) in top of each biscuit; fill each hole with ¼ teaspoon jam.
4 Bake jam drops about 15 minutes; cool on trays.

prep and cook time 45 minutes
makes 24
nutritional count per jam drop 7.3g total fat (3.1g saturated fat); 464kJ (111 cal); 9.3g carbohydrate; 1.8g protein; 0.6g fibre

Honey snap biscuits

80g butter
⅓ cup (115g) honey
½ cup (110g) firmly packed brown sugar
½ teaspoon vanilla extract
¾ cup (110g) plain flour
½ teaspoon ground ginger

1 Preheat the oven to 180°C/160°C fan-assisted. Grease oven trays.
2 Combine butter, honey and sugar in small saucepan; stir over medium heat until butter is melted. Remove from heat, stir in extract.
3 Sift flour and ginger into large bowl; using a wooden spoon, stir in butter mixture, beating until smooth.
4 Drop heaped teaspoons of mixture, about 8cm apart, onto prepared trays, about six at a time; biscuits will spread during cooking.
5 Bake about 8 minutes or until golden brown.
6 Stand biscuits on trays 5 minutes; transfer to wire rack to cool. These biscuits are delicious served with ice-cream or fruit desserts.

prep and cook time 45 minutes
makes about 45
nutritional count per biscuit 1.5g total fat (1g saturated fat); 159kJ (38 cal); 6g carbohydrate; 0.3g protein; 0.1g fibre

Passionfruit melting moments

3 passionfruit
250g butter, softened
1 teaspoon vanilla extract
½ cup (80g) icing sugar
1⅔ cups (250g) plain flour
½ cup (75g) cornflour
passionfruit butter cream
80g butter, softened
⅔ cup (110g) soft icing sugar

1 Preheat oven to 170°C/150°C fan-assisted. Line three baking trays with baking parchment.

2 Remove pulp from passionfruit, place in fine sieve; press down with back of a spoon. Reserve 1 tablespoon of passionfruit juice for passionfruit butter cream.

3 Beat butter, extract and sifted icing sugar in medium bowl with electric mixer until pale. Stir in combined sifted flours in two batches; stir in passionfruit pulp.

4 With lightly floured hands, roll 2 level teaspoons of mixture into balls; place on prepared trays about 3cm apart. Dip fork into a little extra flour, press biscuits lightly.

5 Bake, uncovered, about 15 minutes or until biscuits are a pale straw colour. Cool biscuits on trays 5 minutes; transfer to wire racks to cool.

6 Meanwhile, make passionfruit butter.

7 Sandwich biscuits with 1 teaspoon of the passionfruit butter cream. Dust with a little extra sifted icing sugar, if desired.

passionfruit butter cream Beat butter and sifted icing sugar in small bowl with electric mixer until pale and fluffy. Beat in reserved passionfruit juice.

prep and cook time 55 minutes
makes about 25
nutritional count per melting moment 11g total fat (7.2g saturated fat); 719kJ (172 cal); 17.7g carbohydrate; 1.2g protein; 0.7g fibre

BISCUITS CAN BE MADE A WEEK AHEAD; STORE IN AN AIRTIGHT CONTAINER OR GLASS JAR. SANDWICH WITH PASSIONFRUIT BUTTER CREAM CLOSE TO SERVING.

Chocolate melting moments

125g butter, chopped
2 tablespoons icing sugar
¾ cup (110g) plain flour
2 tablespoons cornflour
2 tablespoons cocoa powder
¼ cup (85g) chocolate hazelnut spread

1 Preheat oven to 180°C/160°C fan-assisted. Lightly grease two baking trays.
2 Beat butter and sugar in small bowl with electric mixer until light and fluffy. Stir in sifted dry ingredients, in two batches.
3 Spoon mixture into piping bag fitted with 5mm fluted tube; pipe directly onto prepared trays, allowing 3cm between each biscuit. Bake, uncovered, about 10 minutes or until biscuits are firm. Stand biscuits 5 minutes; transfer to wire rack to cool.
4 Sandwich biscuits with spread to serve.

prep and cook time 25 minutes
makes 28
nutritional count per melting moment 4.8g total fat (2.8g saturated fat); 293kJ (70 cal); 6.2g carbohydrate; 0.7g protein; 0.2g fibre

STRAWBERRY OR RASPBERRY JAM CAN ALSO BE USED INSTEAD OF THE CHOCOLATE HAZELNUT SPREAD.

Apricot & honey rock cakes

1 cup (160g) wholemeal self-raising flour
1 cup (150g) white self-raising flour
¼ cup (55g) caster sugar
¼ teaspoon ground cinnamon
90g butter, chopped
½ cup (80g) finely chopped dried apricots
2 tablespoons sultanas
1 egg
2 tablespoons honey
⅓ cup (80ml) milk

1 Preheat oven to 200°C/180°C fan-assisted. Grease two oven trays.
2 Sift dry ingredients into large bowl; rub in butter. Stir in apricots and sultanas. Combine egg and honey in small bowl; stir into mixture with milk.
3 Drop tablespoonfuls of the mixture in rough heaps onto trays. Bake, uncovered, about 15 minutes. Cool on trays.

prep and cook time 35 minutes
makes 15
nutritional count per rock cake 5.8g total fat (3.5g saturated fat); 702kJ (168 cal); 24.3g carbohydrate; 3.2g protein; 2.1g fibre

Almond macaroons

2 egg whites
½ cup (110g) caster sugar
1¼ cups (150g) ground almonds
½ teaspoon almond essence
2 tablespoons plain flour
¼ cup (40g) blanched almonds

1 Preheat oven to 150°C/130°C fan-assisted. Grease two oven trays.
2 Beat egg whites in small bowl with electric mixer until soft peaks form. Gradually add sugar, beating until dissolved between additions. Fold in ground almonds, essence and sifted flour, in two batches.
3 Drop level tablespoons of mixture about 5cm apart on trays; press one nut onto each macaroon. Bake about 20 minutes or until firm and dry; cool on trays.

prep and cook time 35 minutes
makes 22
nutritional count per macaroon 4.8g total fat (0.3g saturated fat); 326kJ (78 cal); 6.1g carbohydrate; 2.2g protein; 0.8g fibre

Greek shortbread

250g butter, softened
1 teaspoon vanilla extract
1 cup (220g) caster sugar
1 egg
¼ cup (60ml) brandy
¾ cup (120g) roasted blanched almonds, chopped finely
1½ cups (225g) self-raising flour
2½ cups (375g) plain flour
½ teaspoon ground nutmeg
¼ cup (60ml) rosewater
½ cup (125ml) water
3 cups (480g) icing sugar

1 Preheat oven to 180°C/160°C fan-assisted. Grease oven trays.
2 Beat butter, extract and caster sugar in small bowl with electric mixer until light and fluffy. Beat in egg and brandy; transfer mixture to large bowl. Stir in nuts and sifted flours and nutmeg, in two batches.
3 Turn dough onto floured surface; knead gently until smooth. Shape level tablespoons of the dough into crescent shapes; place about 3cm apart on trays. Bake, uncovered, about 15 minutes or until browned lightly.
4 Lift shortbread onto wire racks; brush hot shortbread with combined rosewater and the water. Coat thickly with sifted icing sugar; cool to room temperature.

prep and cook time 1 hour
makes 50
nutritional count per piece 5.7g total fat (2.8g saturated fat); 644kJ (154 cal); 22.7g carbohydrate; 1.9g protein; 0.7g fibre

THESE DELICIOUS BISCUITS ARE TRADITIONALLY SERVED AT CHRISTMAS IN GREECE, BUT THEY ARE OFTEN SERVED YEAR-ROUND IN CAFES AS THEY ARE TOO GOOD TO HAVE JUST ONCE A YEAR.

Traditional Scottish shortbread

250g butter, softened
⅓ cup (75g) caster sugar
1 tablespoon water
2 cups (300g) plain flour
½ cup (100g) rice flour
2 tablespoons white granulated sugar

1 Preheat oven to 160°C/140°C fan-assisted. Grease oven trays.
2 Beat butter and caster sugar in medium bowl with electric mixer until light and fluffy; stir in the water and sifted flours, in two batches. Knead on floured surface until smooth.
3 Divide dough in half; shape each, on separate trays, into 20cm rounds. Mark each round into 12 wedges; prick with fork. Pinch edges of rounds with fingers; sprinkle with white sugar.
4 Bake shortbread about 40 minutes; stand on trays 5 minutes. Using sharp knife, cut shortbread into wedges along marked lines. Cool on trays.

prep and cook time 1 hour
makes 24
nutritional count per shortbread
8.8g total fat (5.7g saturated fat);
644kJ (154 cal); 17g carbohydrate;
1.7g protein; 0.6g fibre

Let's Eat Outdoors

COLD MEAT TERRINE
country-style

Impossible pie

BANGERS & MASH

old-fashioned
CHICKEN SALAD

IT'S SUMMERTIME AND THE LIVING IS EASY – FILLED WITH PICNICS, BARBECUES AND SWEET, SEASONAL PRODUCE

Grilled sausages with fruit relish

1 tablespoon olive oil
1 small red onion (100g), chopped finely
1 clove garlic, crushed
2 medium pears (460g), chopped finely
¼ cup (55g) finely chopped dried apricots
¼ cup (40g) sultanas, chopped finely
2 tablespoons cider vinegar
2 tablespoons brown sugar
½ teaspoon ground allspice
12 thick pork sausages (1.5kg)

1   Heat oil in medium saucepan; cook onion and garlic, stirring, until onions soften. Add fruit, vinegar, sugar and spice; cook, uncovered, stirring occasionally, about 10 minutes or until mixture is thick and pulpy.
2   Meanwhile, cook sausages on heated oiled grill plate (or grill or barbecue) until cooked through.
3   Serve sausages with fruit relish.

prep and cook time 30 minutes
serves 6
nutritional count per serving 58.7g total fat (22.9g saturated fat); 3252kJ (778 cal); 29.9g carbohydrate; 31g protein; 6.2g fibre

Pea mash

1kg floury potatoes, peeled, coarsely chopped
1½ cups (180g) frozen peas
¾ cup (180ml) hot milk
50g butter, softened

1   Boil, steam or microwave potato and peas, separately, until tender; drain.
2   Mash potato in large bowl; stir in milk and butter.
3   Using fork, mash peas in small bowl; stir into potato mixture until combined.

prep and cook time 30 minutes
serves 4
nutritional count per serving 12.4g total fat (7.9g saturated fat); 1212kJ (290 cal); 34.5g carbohydrate; 9.4g protein; 6.1g fibre

THIS FLAVOUR-PACKED
FRUIT RELISH ADDS A
SOPHISTICATED TOUCH TO
EVERYONE'S TRADITIONAL,
FAVOURITE COMFORT MEAL:
BANGERS AND MASH.

Chicken liver paté with port

500g chicken livers
⅓ cup (80ml) port
120g butter
1 medium white onion (150g), chopped finely
1 clove garlic, crushed
½ teaspoon dried tarragon
2 tablespoons brandy
1 tablespoon tomato paste
⅓ cup (80g) soured cream

1   Trim and wash chicken livers; cut in half. Combine livers in small bowl with port; cover. Stand 2 hours; strain.

2   Melt a quarter of the butter in medium frying pan; cook onion and garlic, stirring constantly over medium heat about 3 minutes or until onion is soft. Add livers to pan; stir constantly about 5 minutes or until livers are just changed in colour. Stir in tarragon and brandy; bring to the boil. Reduce heat; simmer, uncovered, about 3 minutes or until livers are tender.

3   Melt a quarter of the butter in saucepan. Blend or process liver mixture until smooth. Add tomato paste and soured cream; blend until combined. While motor is operating, gradually add melted butter.

4   Pour pâté into four ½-cup (125ml) serving dishes; garnish with sprig of herbs or bay leaf, if desired. Cover; refrigerate 2 hours.

5   Coarsely chop remaining butter; melt in small saucepan over low heat, without stirring. Stand a few minutes, then use spoon to carefully remove and discard whitish-coloured scum floating on surface. Carefully pour remaining clear liquid into jug, leaving whitish milky deposits in the pan; discard deposits.

6   Gently pour a thin layer of clarified butter over pâté; refrigerate overnight.

prep and cook time 40 minutes (plus standing and refrigeration)
serves 10
nutritional count per serving 15g total fat (9.2g saturated fat); 836kJ (200 cal); 3g carbohydrate; 9.7g protein; 0.3g fibre

Country style terrine

350g chicken thigh fillets, chopped coarsely
400g boned pork belly, rind removed, chopped coarsely
300g piece calves liver, trimmed, chopped coarsely
3 bacon rashers (210g), rind removed, chopped coarsely
3 cloves garlic, crushed
2 teaspoons finely chopped fresh thyme
10 juniper berries, crushed
2 tablespoons port
¼ cup (60ml) dry white wine
1 egg
¼ cup (35g) roasted, shelled pistachios

1 Preheat oven to 150°C/130°C fan-assisted. Oil 1.5-litre (6-cup) ovenproof terrine dish.
2 Blend or process meats, separately, until coarsely minced; combine in large bowl with remaining ingredients.
3 Press meat mixture into terrine dish; cover with foil. Place terrine dish in baking dish; add enough boiling water into baking dish to come halfway up side of terrine dish. Bake 1 hour. Uncover; bake a further 1 hour or until cooked through.
4 Remove terrine dish from baking dish; cover terrine with baking parchment. Weight with another dish filled with heavy cans; cool 10 minutes then refrigerate overnight.
5 Turn terrine onto serving plate; serve sliced, at room temperature, with french bread and cornichons, if desired.

prep and cook time 2 hours 20 minutes (plus refrigeration)
serves 6
nutritional count per serving 30.1g total fat (9.6g saturated fat); 2019kJ (483 cal); 3.6g carbohydrate; 46.2g protein; 0.8g fibre

Barbecued lamb chops with mustard & thyme marinade

2 tablespoons olive oil
2 cloves garlic, crushed
2 tablespoons wholegrain mustard
2 tablespoons lemon juice
2 teaspoons finely chopped fresh thyme
4 forequarter lamb chops (760g)

1 Combine oil, garlic, mustard, juice and thyme in large bowl; add chops, turn to coat in marinade. Cover; refrigerate 3 hours or overnight.
2 Cook drained chops on heated oiled grill plate (or grill or barbecue) until browned both sides and cooked as desired.
3 Serve chops, if desired, with vegetables and extra mustard.

prep and cook time 30 minutes (plus refrigeration)
serves 4
nutritional count per serving 17.5g total fat (5.1g saturated fat); 1158kJ (277 cal); 0.8g carbohydrate; 29g protein; 0.5g fibre

Herb salad with dijon vinaigrette

1 green oak leaf lettuce, leaves separated
¼ cup coarsely chopped fresh chives
½ cup firmly packed fresh flat-leaf parsley leaves
½ cup firmly packed fresh chervil leaves
dijon vinaigrette
2 tablespoons olive oil
2 tablespoons white wine vinegar
1 tablespoon dijon mustard
2 teaspoons white sugar

1 Place ingredients for vinaigrette in screw-top jar; shake well. Add dijon vinaigrette to salad ingredients in medium bowl; toss gently to combine.

prep time 10 minutes **serves** 6
nutritional count per serving 6.2g total fat (0.9g saturated fat); 288kJ (69 cal); 2g carbohydrate; 0.7g protein; 1.1g fibre

Corned beef with parsley sauce

1.5kg whole piece beef corned silverside
2 bay leaves
6 black peppercorns
1 large brown onion (200g), quartered
1 large carrot (180g), chopped coarsely
1 tablespoon brown malt vinegar
¼ cup (50g) firmly packed brown sugar
parsley sauce
30g butter
¼ cup (35g) plain flour
2½ cups (625ml) milk
⅓ cup (40g) grated cheddar cheese
⅓ cup finely chopped fresh flat-leaf parsley
1 tablespoon mild mustard

1 Place beef, bay leaves, peppercorns, onion, carrot, vinegar and half of the sugar in large saucepan. Add enough water to just cover beef; simmer, covered, about 2 hours or until beef is tender. Cool beef 1 hour in liquid in pan.
2 Remove beef from pan; discard liquid. Sprinkle sheet of foil with remaining sugar, wrap beef in foil; stand 20 minutes before serving.
3 Make parsley sauce.
4 Serve sliced corned beef with parsley sauce.
parsley sauce Melt butter in small saucepan, add flour; cook, stirring, until bubbling. Gradually stir in milk; cook, stirring, until sauce boils and thickens. Remove from heat; stir in cheese, parsley and mustard.

prep and cook time 2 hours 30 minutes (plus standing and cooling)
serves 4
nutritional count per serving 35.8g total fat (19.3g saturated fat); 3520kJ (842 cal); 31g carbohydrate; 97g protein; 2.5g fibre

Salmon & potato cakes

1kg potatoes, peeled
440g can red salmon
1 small brown onion (80g), chopped finely
1 tablespoon finely chopped fresh flat-leaf parsley
1 teaspoon finely grated lemon rind
1 tablespoon lemon juice
½ cup (75g) plain flour
1 egg
2 tablespoons milk
½ cup (50g) packaged breadcrumbs
½ cup (35g) stale breadcrumbs
vegetable oil, for deep-frying

1 Boil, steam or microwave potatoes until tender; drain. Mash potato in large bowl.
2 Drain salmon; discard any skin and bones. Add salmon to potato with onion, parsley, rind and juice; mix well. Cover; refrigerate 30 minutes.
3 Using floured hands, shape salmon mixture into eight cakes. Toss cakes in flour; shake away excess. Dip cakes, one at a time, in combined egg and milk, then in combined breadcrumbs.
4 Heat oil in wok; deep-fry cakes, in batches, until browned lightly. Drain on absorbent kitchen paper.

prep and cook time 40 minutes (plus refrigeration)
makes 8
nutritional count per cake 16.7g total fat (3.1g saturated fat); 1396kJ (334 cal); 28.6g carbohydrate; 15.9g protein; 2.7g fibre

Quiche lorraine

1¾ cups (255g) plain flour
150g chilled butter, chopped
1 egg yolk
2 teaspoons lemon juice, approx
⅓ cup (80ml) cold water
1 medium brown onion (150g), chopped finely
3 bacon rashers (210g), chopped finely
3 eggs
300ml double cream
½ cup (125ml) milk
¾ cup (120g) grated cheddar cheese

1 Sift flour into bowl; rub in butter. Add egg yolk, juice and enough water to make ingredients cling together. Knead gently on floured surface until smooth. Cover; refrigerate 30 minutes.
2 Preheat oven to 200°C/180°C fan-assisted.
3 Roll pastry between sheets of baking parchment large enough to line a deep 23cm loose-base flan tin. Lift pastry into flan tin; gently ease pastry into side of tin. Trim edge. Place flan on oven tray.
4 Line pastry with baking parchment, fill with dried beans or rice. Bake for 10 minutes; remove paper and beans carefully. Bake pastry about 10 minutes or until golden brown; cool to room temperature.
5 Reduce oven to 180°C/160°C fan-assisted.
6 Cook onion and bacon in oiled small frying pan until onion is soft; drain away excess fat. Cool; sprinkle into pastry case.
7 Whisk eggs in medium bowl; whisk in cream, milk and cheese until just combined. Pour into pastry case.
8 Bake quiche about 35 minutes or until filling is set and brown. Stand 5 minutes before removing from tin.

prep and cook time 1 hour 30 minutes (plus chilling and standing)
serves 6
nutritional count per serving 58.1g total fat (35.4g saturated fat); 3127kJ (748 cal); 34.8g carbohydrate; 22g protein; 1.9g fibre

Easy picnic loaf

3 cups (450g) self-raising flour
30g butter
½ cup (125ml) milk
1 cup (250ml) water, approximately

1 Preheat oven to 180°C/160°C fan-assisted. Grease oven tray.
2 Sift flour into bowl; rub in butter. Make well in centre, add milk and enough water to mix to a soft sticky dough. Knead on floured surface until smooth.
3 Press dough into 15cm circle, place on tray. Cut a cross through dough, about 1cm deep. Brush top with a little extra milk or water; dust with a little extra flour.
4 Bake 30 minutes or until loaf sounds hollow when tapped.

prep and cook time 45 minutes
serves 6
nutritional count per serving 5.8g total fat (3.4g saturated fat); 1292kJ (309 cal); 53.9g carbohydrate; 8.1g protein; 2.9g fibre

Old-fashioned chicken salad

1 litre (4 cups) boiling water
1 litre (4 cups) chicken stock
700g chicken breast fillets
1 long french bread stick, sliced thinly
2 tablespoons olive oil
½ cup (150g) mayonnaise
½ cup (120g) soured cream
2 tablespoons lemon juice
4 trimmed celery stalks (400g), sliced thinly
1 medium white onion (150g), chopped finely
3 large dill pickles (150g), sliced thinly
2 tablespoons finely chopped fresh flat-leaf parsley
1 tablespoon finely chopped tarragon
1 large round lettuce, leaves separated

1 Bring the water and stock to the boil in large frying pan; poach chicken, covered, about 10 minutes or until cooked through. Cool chicken in liquid 10 minutes; slice thinly. Discard liquid.
2 Meanwhile, brush both sides of bread slices with oil; toast under preheated grill until browned lightly both sides.
3 Whisk mayonnaise, cream and juice in small bowl.
4 Place chicken in large bowl with celery, onion, pickle and herbs; toss gently to combine.
5 Place lettuce leaves on serving platter; top with salad and bread, drizzle with mayonnaise mixture.

prep and cook time 50 minutes serves 4
nutritional count per serving 41g total fat (12.5g saturated fat); 3323kJ (795 cal); 52g carbohydrate; 51.7g protein; 6.4g fibre

Potato salad

2kg potatoes, peeled
2 tablespoons cider vinegar
8 spring onions, sliced thinly
¼ cup finely chopped fresh flat-leaf parsley
mayonnaise
2 egg yolks
1 teaspoon dijon mustard
2 teaspoons lemon juice
1 cup (250ml) vegetable oil
2 tablespoons hot water, approximately

1 Cut potatoes into 1.5cm pieces. Place potato in large saucepan, barely cover with cold water; cover saucepan, bring to the boil. Reduce heat; simmer, uncovered, stirring occasionally, until just tender. Drain, spread potato on a tray; sprinkle with vinegar. Cool 10 minutes. Cover; refrigerate until cold.
2 Meanwhile, make mayonnaise.
3 Place potato in large bowl with mayonnaise, onion and parsley; mix gently to combine.
mayonnaise Blend or process egg yolks, mustard and juice until smooth. With motor operating, gradually add oil in a thin, steady stream; process until mixture thickens. Add as much of the hot water as needed to thin mayonnaise.

prep and cook time 40 minutes (plus refrigeration)
serves 8
nutritional count per serving 30.4g total fat (4.1g saturated fat); 1739kJ (416 cal); 28.4g carbohydrate; 6.1g protein; 3.7g fibre

Berry frangipane tart

1 sheet ready-rolled sweet puff pastry
300g frozen mixed berries
frangipane
80g butter, softened
½ teaspoon vanilla extract
⅓ cup (75g) caster sugar
2 egg yolks
1 tablespoon plain flour
1 cup (120g) ground almonds

1 Preheat oven to 220°C/200°C fan-assisted. Grease 20cm x 30cm baking tin.
2 Roll pastry until large enough to cover base and sides of tin; line tin with pastry, press into sides. Prick pastry all over with fork; freeze 5 minutes.
3 Place another baking tin on top of pastry; bake 5 minutes. Remove top tin; bake further 5 minutes or until pastry is browned lightly. Cool 5 minutes.
4 Reduce oven to 180°C/160°C fan-assisted.
5 Meanwhile, make frangipane.
6 Spread frangipane over pastry base. Sprinkle with berries, press into frangipane. Bake about 30 minutes or until browned lightly.
frangipane Beat butter, extract, sugar and egg yolks in small bowl with electric mixer until light and fluffy. Stir in flour and ground almonds.

prep and cook time 50 minutes
serves 6
nutritional count per serving 30.2g total fat (11.9g saturated fat); 1722kJ (412 cal); 26.4g carbohydrate; 7.7g protein; 3.3g fibre

Impossible pie

½ cup (75g) plain flour
1 cup (220g) caster sugar
¾ cup (60g) desiccated coconut
4 eggs
1 teaspoon vanilla extract
125g butter, melted
½ cup (40g) flaked almonds
2 cups (500ml) milk

1 Preheat oven to 180°C/160°C fan-assisted. Grease deep 24cm pie dish.
2 Combine sifted flour, sugar, coconut, eggs, extract, butter and half the nuts in large bowl; gradually add milk, stirring, until combined. Pour mixture into dish.
3 Bake pie 35 minutes. Remove pie from oven, sprinkle remaining nuts over pie; bake 10 minutes. Serve pie with cream or fruit, if desired.

prep and cook time 55 minutes
serves 8
nutritional count per serving 25.7g total fat (15.4g saturated fat); 1747kJ (418 cal); 38.2g carbohydrate; 8.1g protein; 1.9g fibre

THIS MAGICAL DESSERT OBLIGINGLY SORTS ITSELF OUT IN THE OVEN INTO THREE LAYERS, HENCE ITS NAME.

Soured cream cheesecake

250g digestive biscuits
150g butter, melted
250g packet cream cheese, softened
250g cottage cheese
3 eggs
1 cup (220g) caster sugar
2 tablespoons cornflour
½ cup (125ml) milk
1 cup (240g) soured cream
1 tablespoon finely grated lemon rind
1 teaspoon lemon juice

1 Preheat oven to 180°C/160°C fan-assisted.
2 Blend or process biscuits until mixture resembles fine breadcrumbs. Add butter; process until combined. Press biscuit mixture evenly over base and side of 20cm springform tin, place on oven tray; refrigerate about 30 minutes or until firm.
3 Meanwhile, beat cheeses together until smooth. Beat in eggs, one at a time. Stir in sugar and cornflour then milk, cream, rind and juice. Pour into crumb crust.
4 Bake cheesecake about 50 minutes. Cool in oven with door ajar. Refrigerate overnight.

prep and cook time 1 hour 20 minutes (plus refrigeration)
serves 8
nutritional count per serving 45.3g total fat (28.1g saturated fat); 2704kJ (54.5 cal); 54.5g carbohydrate; 8.5g protein; 0.7g fibre

Lemon meringue pie

½ cup (75g) cornflour
1 cup (220g) caster sugar
½ cup (125ml) lemon juice
1¼ cups (310ml) water
2 teaspoons finely grated lemon rind
60g unsalted butter, chopped
3 eggs, separated
½ cup (110g) caster sugar, extra
pastry
1½ cups (225g) plain flour
1 tablespoon icing sugar
140g chilled butter, chopped
1 egg yolk
2 tablespoons cold water

1 Make pastry.
2 Grease 24cm-round loose-based fluted flan tin. Roll pastry between sheets of baking parchment until large enough to line tin. Ease pastry into tin, press into base and side; trim edge. Cover; refrigerate 30 minutes.
3 Preheat oven to 240°C/220°C fan-assisted.
4 Place tin on oven tray. Line pastry case with baking parchment; fill with dried beans or rice. Bake 15 minutes; remove paper and beans. Bake about 10 minutes; cool pie shell, turn oven off.
5 Meanwhile, combine cornflour and sugar in medium saucepan; gradually stir in juice and the water until smooth. Cook, stirring, over high heat, until mixture boils and thickens. Reduce heat; simmer, stirring, 1 minute. Remove from heat; stir in rind, butter and egg yolks. Cool 10 minutes.
6 Spread lemon filling into pie shell. Cover; refrigerate 2 hours.
7 Preheat oven to 240°C/220°C fan-assisted.
8 Beat egg whites in small bowl with electric mixer until soft peaks form; gradually add extra sugar, beating until sugar dissolves.
9 Roughen surface of filling with fork before spreading with meringue mixture. Bake about 2 minutes or until browned lightly.
pastry Process flour, icing sugar and butter until crumbly. Add egg yolk and the water; process until ingredients come together. Knead dough on floured surface until smooth. Cover; refrigerate 30 minutes.

prep and cook time 1 hour (plus refrigeration)
serves 10
nutritional count per serving 18.9g total fat (11.6g saturated fat); 1772kJ (424 cal); 57.7g carbohydrate; 5g protein; 0.9g fibre

THE TARTNESS OF THIS PIE
DEPENDS ON THE LEMONS YOU
USE AND THE FLAVOUR WILL
VARY SLIGHTLY EVERY TIME
YOU MAKE THE FILLING. WHEN
SIMMERING THE BOILED AND
THICKENED FILLING, YOU MUST
STIR CONTINUALLY: IT'S THICK
AND WILL BURN IF YOU'RE NOT
CAREFUL.

Sunday Lunch

Creamy soups

CLASSIC ROASTS
with all the trimmings

OLD-FASHIONED
rice pudding

FRUITY PIES

A TRADITIONAL ROAST, A
THREE-COURSE MEAL, AND
A LEISURELY PACE. IT'S A WISE
WAY TO SPEND A DAY OF REST

Chicken & vegetable soup

1.5kg whole chicken
1 small brown onion (80g), halved
2 litres (8 cups) water
5 black peppercorns
2 bay leaves
20g butter
2 trimmed celery stalks (200g), sliced thinly
2 medium carrots (240g), cut into 1cm pieces
1 large potato (300g), cut into 1cm pieces
150g mangetout, trimmed, chopped coarsely
3 spring onions, sliced thinly
310g can corn kernels, drained

1 Place chicken, brown onion, the water, peppercorns and bay leaves in large saucepan; bring to the boil. Reduce heat; simmer, covered, 2 hours.
2 Remove chicken from pan. Strain broth through colander into large bowl; discard solids. Allow broth to cool, cover; refrigerate overnight. When chicken is cool enough to handle, remove and discard skin and bones. Shred meat coarsely; cover, refrigerate overnight.
3 Heat butter in same cleaned pan; cook celery, carrot and potato, stirring, until onion softens. Skim and discard fat from surface of broth. Add to pan; bring to the boil. Reduce heat; simmer, covered, about 10 minutes or until vegetables are just tender.
4 Add mangetout, spring onion, corn and reserved chicken to soup; cook, covered, 5 minutes or until heated through.

prep and cook time 2 hours 40 minutes (plus refrigeration)
serves 6
nutritional count per serving 9.2g total fat (2.8g saturated fat); 1183kJ (283 cal); 18.8g carbohydrate; 29.1g protein; 4.2g fibre

Cream of pumpkin soup

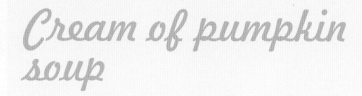

40g butter
1 large brown onion (200g), chopped coarsely
3 bacon rashers (210g), chopped coarsely
1.5kg pumpkin (or butternut squash), chopped coarsely
2 large potatoes (600g), chopped coarsely
1.25 litres (5 cups) chicken stock
½ cup (125ml) double cream

1   Melt butter in large saucepan; cook onion and bacon, stirring, until onion softens. Stir in pumpkin and potato.
2   Stir in stock, bring to the boil; simmer, uncovered, about 20 minutes or until pumpkin is soft.
3   Blend or process soup, in batches, until smooth. Return soup to same cleaned pan, add cream; stir until heated through.

prep and cook time 40 minutes
serves 6
nutritional count per serving 20.9g total fat (12.3g saturated fat); 1555kJ (372 cal); 28g carbohydrate; 16.2g protein; 4.2g fibre

Leek & potato soup

2 medium potatoes (400g), chopped coarsely
2 medium carrots (240g), chopped coarsely
1 large brown onion (200g), chopped coarsely
1 medium tomato (150g), chopped coarsely
1 trimmed celery stalk (100g), chopped coarsely
1.5 litres (6 cups) water
1 tablespoon olive oil
50g butter
4 medium potatoes (800g), chopped coarsely, extra
1 large leek (500g), sliced thickly
300ml double cream
2 tablespoons finely chopped fresh chives
1 tablespoon finely chopped fresh basil
1 tablespoon finely chopped fresh dill

1 Combine potato, carrot, onion, tomato, celery and the water in large saucepan; bring to the boil. Reduce heat; simmer, uncovered, 20 minutes. Strain broth through muslin-lined sieve or colander into large heatproof bowl; discard solids.

2 Heat oil and butter in same cleaned pan; cook extra potato and leek, covered, 15 minutes, stirring occasionally. Add broth; bring to the boil. Reduce heat; simmer, covered, 15 minutes. Cool 15 minutes.

3 Blend or process soup, in batches, until smooth. Return soup to same cleaned pan, add cream; stir over medium heat until hot.

4 Serve soup sprinkled with combined herbs and, if desired, topped with croûtons.

prep and cook time 1 hour 20 minutes (plus cooling)
serves 4
nutritional count per serving 47.9g total fat (28.8g saturated fat); 2822kJ (675 cal); 46.3g carbohydrate; 11g protein; 9.8g fibre

Roast lamb dinner

2kg lamb leg
3 sprigs fresh rosemary, chopped coarsely
½ teaspoon sweet paprika
1kg potatoes, chopped coarsely
500g piece pumpkin (or butternut squash), chopped coarsely
1 large onion (200g), cut into wedges
2 tablespoons olive oil
2 tablespoons plain flour
1 cup (250ml) chicken stock
¼ cup (60ml) dry red wine
cauliflower mornay
1 small cauliflower (1kg), cut into florets
50g butter
¼ cup (35g) plain flour
2 cups (500ml) milk
¾ cup (90g) coarsely grated cheddar cheese

1   Make mint sauce (see right).
2   Meanwhile, preheat oven to 200ºC/180ºC fan-assisted. Place lamb in large oiled baking dish; using sharp knife, score skin at 2cm intervals, sprinkle with rosemary and paprika. Roast, uncovered, 15 minutes.
3   Reduce oven to 180ºC/160ºC fan-assisted. Roast lamb, uncovered, further 45 minutes or until cooked as desired.
4   Meanwhile, place potato, pumpkin and onion, in single layer, in large shallow baking dish; drizzle with oil. Roast, uncovered, for last 45 minutes of lamb cooking time.
5   Make cauliflower mornay.
6   Remove lamb and vegetables from oven; cover to keep warm. Strain pan juices from lamb into medium jug. Return ¼ cup of the pan juices to flameproof dish over medium heat, add flour; cook, stirring, about 5 minutes or until mixture bubbles and browns. Gradually add stock and wine; cook over high heat, stirring, until gravy boils and thickens.
7   Strain gravy; serve with sliced lamb, roasted vegetables, cauliflower mornay and mint sauce.
cauliflower mornay Boil, steam or microwave cauliflower until tender; drain. Melt butter in medium saucepan, add flour; cook, stirring, until mixture bubbles and thickens. Gradually add milk; cook, stirring, until mixture boils and thickens. Stir in half of the cheese. Preheat grill. Place cauliflower in 1.5-litre (6-cup) shallow flameproof dish; pour sauce over cauliflower, sprinkle with remaining cheese. Place under preheated grill about 10 minutes or until browned lightly.

prep and cook time 2 hours (plus standing)
serves 6
nutritional count per serving 35.6g total fat (17g saturated fat); 3244kJ (776 cal); 40.5g carbohydrate; 71.9g protein; 7g fibre

mint sauce

¾ cup (180ml) white vinegar
¼ cup (60ml) water
¼ cup (55g) caster sugar
2 cups coarsely chopped fresh mint

1   Stir vinegar, the water and sugar in small saucepan over heat, without boiling, until sugar dissolves.
2   Combine vinegar mixture and half of the mint in small heatproof bowl, cover; stand 3 hours.
3   Strain mixture into bowl; discard mint. Stir remaining fresh mint into sauce; blend or process until chopped finely.

makes 1 cup mint sauce
nutritional count per tablespoon sauce 0g total fat (0g saturated fat); 96kJ (23 cal); 5g carbohydrate; 0.3g protein; 0.6g fibre

Pork leg roast with sage potatoes

2.5kg boneless pork leg roast, rind on
2 tablespoons olive oil
1 tablespoon sea salt flakes
6 medium potatoes (1.2kg), quartered
2 tablespoons olive oil, extra
2 tablespoons fresh sage leaves
2 tablespoons fresh rosemary leaves
apple sauce
3 large green apples (600g)
¼ cup (60ml) water
1 teaspoon white sugar
pinch ground cinnamon

1 Preheat oven to 220°C/200°C fan-assisted.
2 Score pork rind with sharp knife; rub with oil, then salt. Place pork in large shallow baking dish. Roast, uncovered, 20 minutes.
3 Reduce oven to 180°C/160°C fan-assisted. Roast, uncovered, about 2 hours.
4 Meanwhile, combine potato with extra oil and herbs in large bowl. Place in single layer on oven tray. Roast, uncovered, about 35 minutes.
5 Make apple sauce.
6 Stand pork, covered loosely with foil, 10 minutes before slicing. Serve pork and sage potatoes with apple sauce.
apple sauce Peel and core apples; slice thickly. Place apples and the water in medium saucepan; simmer, uncovered, about 10 minutes or until apple is soft. Remove pan from heat; stir in sugar and cinnamon.

prep and cook time 2 hours 40 minutes (plus standing)
serves 8
nutritional count per serving 34g total fat (9.7g saturated fat); 2976kJ (712 cal); 27.4g carbohydrate; 71.9g protein; 4.1g fibre

Standing rib roast with roast vegetables

1.2kg beef standing rib roast
¼ cup (60ml) olive oil
2 teaspoons cracked black pepper
500g tiny new potatoes
500g pumpkin, chopped coarsely
500g sweet potatoes, chopped coarsely
½ cup (125ml) brandy
1½ cups (375ml) beef stock
1 tablespoon cornflour
¼ cup (60ml) water
1 tablespoon finely chopped fresh chives

1 Preheat oven to 200°C/180°C fan-assisted.
2 Brush beef with 1 tablespoon of the oil; sprinkle with pepper. Heat 1 tablespoon of the oil in large shallow flameproof baking dish; cook beef, uncovered, over high heat until browned all over. Roast, uncovered, in oven about 45 minutes or until cooked as desired.
3 Meanwhile, heat remaining oil in another large flameproof baking dish; cook potatoes, stirring, over high heat until browned lightly. Add pumpkin and sweet potatoes, place dish in oven with beef; roast, uncovered, about 35 minutes or until vegetables are browned.
4 Place beef on vegetables, cover; return to oven to keep warm. Drain juices from beef baking dish into medium saucepan, add brandy; bring to the boil. Add stock and blended cornflour and water; cook, stirring, until sauce boils and thickens slightly. Stir in chives; pour into medium heatproof jug.
5 Serve beef and vegetables with sauce.

prep and cook time 1 hour 50 minutes
serves 4
nutritional count per serving 29.2g total fat (8.5g saturated fat); 3114kJ (745 cal); 41.1g carbohydrate; 60.4g protein; 5.4g fibre

Roast chicken

1.5kg chicken
15g butter, melted
herb stuffing
1½ cups (105g) stale breadcrumbs
1 trimmed celery stalk (100g), chopped finely
1 small white onion (80g), chopped finely
2 teaspoons finely chopped fresh sage leaves
1 tablespoon finely chopped fresh flat-leaf parsley
1 egg, beaten lightly
30g butter, melted

1 Preheat oven to 200°C/180°C fan-assisted.
2 Make herb stuffing.
3 Remove and discard any fat from cavity of chicken. Fill cavity of chicken with stuffing, fold over skin to enclose stuffing; secure with toothpicks. Tie legs together with string.
4 Place chicken on rack over baking dish. Half-fill baking dish with water – it should not touch the chicken. Brush chicken with butter; roast 15 minutes.
5 Reduce oven 180°C/160°C fan-assisted. Bake further 1½ hours or until chicken is cooked through, basting occasionally with pan juices. Stand 10 minutes before breaking or carving into serving-sized pieces.
herb stuffing Combine ingredients together in medium bowl.

prep and cook time 2 hours 15 minutes
serves 4
nutritional count per serving 35.9g total fat (14.4g saturated fat); 2437kJ (583 cal); 19.4g carbohydrate; 45g protein; 1.9g fibre

Roasted root vegetables

2 tablespoons olive oil
12 baby carrots (240g), peeled, halved lengthways
3 small parsnips (180g), peeled, quartered lengthways
12 baby potatoes (480g), halved
4 baby onions (100g), halved
1 clove garlic, crushed
1 tablespoon coarsely chopped fresh rosemary sprigs
1 tablespoon honey
2 teaspoons wholegrain mustard
1 tablespoon lemon juice

1   Preheat oven to 220°C/200°C fan-assisted.
2   Heat oil in large flameproof baking dish; cook carrot, parsnip, potato and onion, stirring, until browned lightly. Remove from heat; stir in garlic, rosemary, honey and mustard.
3   Bake about 25 minutes or until vegetables are tender. Serve drizzled with lemon juice.

prep and cook time 50 minutes
serves 4
nutritional count per serving 4.9g total fat (0.6g saturated fat); 798kJ (191 cal); 29.3g carbohydrate; 4.5g protein; 5.3g fibre

Lamb shank stew

8 french-trimmed lamb shanks (1.6kg)
8 cloves garlic, halved
2 medium lemons (280g)
2 tablespoons olive oil
3 large brown onions (600g), chopped coarsely
2 cups (500ml) dry red wine
3 medium carrots (360g), quartered lengthways
3 trimmed celery stalks (300g), chopped coarsely
4 bay leaves
8 sprigs fresh thyme
1.75 litres (7 cups) chicken stock
½ cup finely chopped fresh flat-leaf parsley
¼ cup finely chopped fresh mint
2kg potatoes, chopped coarsely
300ml double cream
100g butter

1 Pierce meatiest part of each shank in two places with sharp knife; press garlic into cuts.
2 Grate rind of both lemons finely; reserve. Halve lemons; rub cut sides all over shanks.
3 Preheat oven to 180°C/160°C fan-assisted.
4 Heat oil in large flameproof casserole dish; cook shanks, in batches, over heat until browned. Cook onion, stirring, in same dish until softened. Add wine; bring to the boil, then remove dish from heat.
5 Place carrot, celery and shanks, in alternate layers, on onion mixture in dish. Top with bay leaves and thyme; carefully pour stock over the top. Cover dish tightly with lid or foil; cook in oven about 3 hours or until meat is tender.
6 Combine reserved grated rind and herbs in bowl.
7 Boil, steam or microwave potato until tender; drain. Mash potato with warmed cream and butter in large bowl until smooth. Cover to keep warm.
8 Transfer shanks to platter; cover to keep warm. Strain pan juices through muslin-lined sieve into medium saucepan; discard solids. Boil pan juices, uncovered, stirring occasionally, until reduced by half.
9 Divide mashed potato among plates; top with shanks, sprinkle with rind-herb mixture, drizzle with pan juices. Serve with green beans, if desired.

prep and cook time 3 hours 20 minutes
serves 8
nutritional count per serving 34.3g total fat (19.5g saturated fat); 2721kJ (651 cal); 37.8g carbohydrate; 34.3g protein; 7.4g fibre

Spiced apricot & plum pie

2 x 825g cans dark plums in light syrup
2 cups (300g) dried apricots
1 cinnamon stick
3 cloves
½ teaspoon mixed spice
½ teaspoon ground ginger
2 sheets ready-rolled puff pastry
1 egg, beaten lightly
icing sugar, for dusting
spiced yogurt cream
½ cup (140g) natural yogurt
½ cup (120g) soured cream
1 tablespoon ground cinnamon
¼ teaspoon ground ginger

1 Preheat oven to 200°C/180°C fan-assisted. Grease deep 1.25 litre (5-cup) rectangular dish or 26cm pie dish.

2 Drain plums; reserve 1 cup of the syrup. Halve plums, discard stones; place plums in dish.

3 Combine reserved syrup, apricots, cinnamon, cloves, mixed spice and ginger in medium saucepan; simmer, uncovered, until liquid is reduced to ½ cup. Remove and discard cinnamon stick and cloves; cool to room temperature. Pour mixture over plums.

4 Cut pastry into 2.5cm strips. Brush edges of dish with a little of the egg; press pastry strips around edges of dish. Twist remaining strips, place over filling in a lattice pattern; trim ends, brush top with remaining egg.

5 Bake pie about 40 minutes or until pastry is browned lightly.

6 Make spiced yogurt cream.

7 Dust pie generously with icing sugar; serve with the spiced yogurt cream.

spiced yogurt cream Combine ingredients in small bowl.

prep and cook time 1 hour 10 minutes (plus cooling)
serves 8
nutritional count per serving 16.9g total fat (9.6g saturated fat); 1751kJ (419 cal); 57.1g carbohydrate; 6.4g protein; 6.3g fibre

Rice pudding

½ cup (100g) uncooked white medium-grain rice
2½ cups (625ml) milk
¼ cup (55g) caster sugar
¼ cup (40g) sultanas
½ teaspoon vanilla extract
2 teaspoons butter
½ teaspoon ground nutmeg

1 Preheat oven to 160°C/140°C fan-assisted. Grease shallow 1-litre (4-cup) baking dish.
2 Wash rice under cold water; drain well. Place rice, milk, sugar, sultanas and extract in dish; whisk lightly with fork. Dot with butter.
3 Bake rice, uncovered, 1 hour, whisking lightly with fork under skin occasionally. Sprinkle with nutmeg; bake further 20 minutes. Serve warm or cold.

prep and cook time 1 hour 20 minutes
serves 6
nutritional count per serving 5.5g total fat (3.6g saturated fat); 840kJ (201 cal); 32.4g carbohydrate; 4.8g protein; 0.4g fibre

NUTMEG IS A PUNGENT SPICE GROUND FROM THE NUT OF AN INDONESIAN EVERGREEN TREE. USUALLY PURCHASED GROUND, THE FLAVOUR IS MORE INTENSE IF YOU GRATE IT FRESH FROM THE WHOLE NUT USING A FINE GRATER.

Apple pie with passionfruit icing

8 medium (1.5kg) apples
⅔ cup (150g) caster sugar
½ cup (125ml) water
2 tablespoons white sugar, optional
pastry
3 cups (450g) self-raising flour
¼ cup (40g) icing sugar
125g chilled butter, chopped coarsely
1 egg, beaten lightly
½ cup (125ml) milk, approximately
passionfruit icing
½ cups (240g) icing sugar
2 passionfruit

1 Peel, quarter and core apples; slice thickly. Place apples, caster sugar and the water in large saucepan; cover, bring to the boil, reduce heat, simmer about 10 minutes or until the apples are just tender. Gently turn the apple mixture into a large colander or strainer to drain; cool to room temperature.
2 Preheat oven to 200°C/180°C fan-assisted. Grease 20cm x 30cm baking tin; line base with baking parchment, extending paper 5cm over two long sides.
3 Make pastry.
4 Roll two-thirds of the pastry on floured surface until large enough to line base and sides of tin, with 1cm extending over sides. Lift pastry into tin. Spread cold apple mixture into pastry case; brush edges with a little extra milk. Roll out remaining pastry until large enough to generously cover pie. Place over filling; press edges together to seal. Trim excess pastry around edges. Brush top with a little milk; sprinkle with white sugar. Slash about six holes in pastry.
5 Bake pie 45 minutes. Stand in tin 10 minutes; turn, right-side up, on wire rack to cool.
6 Meanwhile, make passionfruit icing. Spread icing over pastry; serve cut into squares.
pastry Sift flour and icing sugar into large bowl; rub in butter. Make a well in centre. Using a knife, 'cut' combined egg and enough milk through flour mixture to make a soft dough.
passionfruit icing Sift icing sugar into medium heatproof bowl, stir in passionfruit pulp, then enough water to make a stiff paste. Place bowl over saucepan of simmering water; stir icing until spreadable.

prep and cook time 1 hour 40 minutes (plus cooling)
serves 8
nutritional count per serving 14.9g total fat (9.2g saturated fat); 2658kJ (636 cal); 114.1g carbohydrate; 7.6g protein; 5.3g fibre

Rhubarb & pear sponge pudding

825g can pear slices in natural juice
800g rhubarb, trimmed, cut into 4cm pieces
2 tablespoons caster sugar
2 eggs
⅓ cup (75g) caster sugar, extra
2 tablespoons plain flour
2 tablespoons self-raising flour
2 tablespoons cornflour

1 Preheat oven to 180°C/160°C fan-assisted.

2 Drain pears; reserve ¾ cup (180ml) of the juice.

3 Place reserved juice, rhubarb and sugar in large saucepan; cook, stirring occasionally, about 5 minutes or until rhubarb is just tender. Stir in pears. Pour mixture into deep 1.75-litre (7-cup) ovenproof dish.

4 Meanwhile, beat eggs in small bowl with electric mixer until thick and creamy. Gradually add extra sugar, 1 tablespoon at a time, beating until sugar dissolves between additions. Gently fold in combined sifted flours.

5 Spread sponge mixture over hot rhubarb mixture. Bake about 45 minutes or until browned lightly and cooked through.

prep and cook time 1 hour 10 minutes
serves 6
nutritional count per serving 2.1g total fat (0.6g saturated fat); 823kJ (197 cal); 35.7g carbohydrate; 5.4g protein; 5.9g fibre

Lemon delicious pudding

125g butter, melted
2 teaspoons finely grated lemon rind
1½ cups (330g) caster sugar
3 eggs, separated
½ cup (75g) self-raising flour
⅓ cup (80ml) lemon juice
1⅓ cups (330ml) milk

1 Preheat oven to 180°C/160°C fan-assisted. Grease six 1-cup (250ml) ovenproof dishes.
2 Combine butter, rind, sugar and yolks in large bowl. Stir in sifted flour then juice. Gradually stir in milk; mixture should be smooth and runny.
3 Beat egg whites in small bowl with electric mixer until soft peaks form; fold into lemon mixture, in two batches.
4 Place ovenproof dishes in large baking dish; divide lemon mixture among dishes. Add enough boiling water to baking dish to come halfway up sides of ovenproof dishes. Bake, uncovered, about 45 minutes.

prep and cook time 1 hour
serves 6
nutritional count per serving 22g total fat (13.5g saturated fat); 2069kJ (495 cal); 67.1g carbohydrate; 6.7g protein; 0.5g fibre

See you for Tea!

DAINTY SANDWICHES
with crusts cut off

WARM SCONES

featherlight
SPONGE CAKE

Spicy teacake

IT'S GOOD TO KNOW YOU CAN ALWAYS RELY ON YOUR FRIENDS AND THE GENTLE ART OF FRESHLY-BAKED AFTERNOON TEA

Basic scones

2½ cups (375g) self-raising flour
1 tablespoon caster sugar
¼ teaspoon salt
30g butter
¾ cup (180ml) milk
½ cup (125ml) water, approximately

1 Preheat oven to 220°C/200°C fan-assisted. Grease deep 19cm-square cake tin.

2 Sift flour, sugar and salt into large bowl; rub in butter with fingertips.

3 Make well in centre of flour mixture; add milk and almost all of the water. Using a knife, 'cut' the milk and the water through the flour mixture to mix to a soft, sticky dough. Add remaining water only if needed. Knead dough on floured surface until smooth.

4 Use hand to press dough out evenly to 2cm thickness. Cut as many 4.5cm rounds as you can from dough. Place rounds side by side, just touching, in tin. Gently knead scraps of dough together; repeat pressing and cutting of dough, place in same tin. Brush tops with a little extra milk.

5 Bake scones about 15 minutes or until browned and scones sound hollow when tapped firmly on the top with fingers.

prep and cook time 45 minutes
makes 16
nutritional count per scone 2.3g total fat (1.3g saturated fat); 443kJ (106 cal); 18.2g carbohydrate; 2.7g protein; 0.9g fibre

Variation

date scones When making the basic scone mixture, stir ¾ cup (120g) finely chopped pitted dried dates into the flour mixture after the butter has been rubbed in. Also, replace the milk and water with 1¼ cups (310ml) buttermilk.

prep and cook time 45 minutes
makes 16
nutritional count per scone 2.4g total fat (1.3g saturated fat); 552kJ (132 cal); 21.7g carbohydrate; 3.8g protein; 3.4g fibre

Pumpkin scones

40g butter
¼ cup (55g) caster sugar
1 egg, beaten lightly
¾ cup cooked mashed pumpkin (or butternut squash)
2½ cups (375g) self-raising flour
½ teaspoon ground nutmeg
⅓ cup (180ml) milk, approximately

1   Preheat oven to 220°C/200°C fan-assisted. Grease two 20cm-round sandwich tins.
2   Beat butter and sugar in small bowl with electric mixer until light and fluffy; beat in egg.
3   Transfer mixture to large bowl. Stir in pumpkin, then sifted dry ingredients and enough milk to make a soft sticky dough. Knead dough on floured surface until smooth.
4   Use hand to press dough out evenly to 2cm thickness. Cut as many 5cm rounds as you can from dough. Place rounds side by side, just touching, in tins. Gently knead scraps of dough together; repeat pressing and cutting of dough, place in same tins. Brush tops with a little extra milk.
5   Bake scones about 15 minutes or until browned and scones sound hollow when tapped firmly on the top with fingers.

prep and cook time 35 minutes
makes 16
nutritional count per scone 2.9g total fat (1.7g saturated fat); 527kJ (126 cal); 21.1g carbohydrate; 3.2g protein; 1.1g fibre

Finger sandwiches

Prosciutto, blue brie & fig

50g blue brie, softened
8 slices light rye bread
6 slices prosciutto (90g), halved widthways
4 medium figs (240g), sliced thinly

1 Spread cheese over four bread slices; top with prosciutto, fig and remaining bread.
2 Remove and discard crusts; cut sandwiches into three strips.

prep time 10 minutes
makes 12
nutritional count per finger 2.5g total fat (1.1g saturated fat); 368kJ (88 cal); 12g carbohydrate; 4.5g protein; 1.9g fibre

Chicken, capers & mayonnaise

2 cups (320g) coarsely shredded cooked chicken
2 tablespoons drained capers, chopped coarsely
2 tablespoons finely chopped fresh chives
⅓ cup (100g) whole-egg mayonnaise
8 slices brown bread
½ cucumber (130g), sliced thinly

1 Combine chicken, capers, chives and ¼ cup of the mayonnaise in medium bowl.
2 Spread chicken mixture over four bread slices; top with cucumber. Spread remaining mayonnaise over remaining bread; place on top of cucumber.
3 Remove and discard crusts; cut sandwiches into three strips.

prep time 10 minutes
makes 12
nutritional count per finger 4.3g total fat (0.7g saturated fat); 422kJ (101 cal); 9.9g carbohydrate; 5.7g protein; 1.2g fibre

Hummingbird cake

You need approximately 2 large overripe bananas (460g) for this recipe.

450g can crushed pineapple in syrup
1 cup (150g) plain flour
½ cup (75g) self-raising flour
½ teaspoon bicarbonate of soda
½ teaspoon ground cinnamon
½ teaspoon ground ginger
1 cup (200g) firmly packed brown sugar
½ cup (45g) desiccated coconut
1 cup mashed banana
2 eggs, beaten lightly
¾ cup (180ml) vegetable oil
cream cheese frosting
30g butter, softened
60g cream cheese, softened
1 teaspoon vanilla extract
1½ cups (240g) icing sugar

1 Preheat oven to 180°C/160°C fan-assisted. Grease deep 23cm-square cake tin, line base with baking parchment.
2 Drain pineapple over medium bowl, pressing with spoon to extract as much syrup as possible. Reserve ¼ cup (60ml) syrup.
3 Sift flours, soda, spices and sugar into large bowl. Using wooden spoon, stir in drained pineapple, reserved syrup, coconut, banana, egg and oil; pour into tin.
4 Bake cake about 40 minutes. Stand in tin 5 minutes; turn, top-side up, on wire rack to cool.
5 Meanwhile, make cream cheese frosting. Spread cold cake with frosting before serving.
cream cheese frosting Beat butter, cream cheese and extract in small bowl with electric mixer until light and fluffy; gradually beat in icing sugar.

prep and cook time 1 hour 10 minutes
serves 12
nutritional count per serving 21.1g total fat (6.6g saturated fat); 1881kJ (450 cal); 59.5g carbohydrate; 4.5g protein; 2.2g fibre

THIS MOIST, LUSCIOUS CAKE FROM THE AMERICAN DEEP SOUTH TRANSLATES AS DELICIOUS IN ANYONE'S LANGUAGE. MAKE SURE YOU DRAIN THE PINEAPPLE THOROUGHLY FOR THIS RECIPE OTHERWISE THE CAKE WILL BE SOGGY.

Carrot cake with lemon cream cheese frosting

3 eggs
1⅓ cups (250g) firmly packed brown sugar
1 cup (250ml) vegetable oil
3 cups firmly packed, coarsely grated carrot
1 cup (120g) coarsely chopped walnuts
2½ cups (375g) self-raising flour
½ teaspoon bicarbonate of soda
2 teaspoons mixed spice
lemon cream cheese frosting
30g butter, softened
80g cream cheese, softened
1 teaspoon finely grated lemon rind
1½ cups (240g) icing sugar

You need approximately 3 large carrots (540g) for this recipe.

1 Preheat oven to 180°C/160°C fan-assisted. Grease deep 22cm-round cake tin, line base with baking parchment.
2 Beat eggs, sugar and oil in small bowl with electric mixer until thick and creamy. Transfer mixture to large bowl; stir in carrot and nuts then sifted dry ingredients. Pour mixture into tin.
3 Bake cake about 1¼ hours. Stand in tin 5 minutes; turn, top-side up, onto wire rack to cool.
4 Meanwhile, make lemon cream cheese frosting. Spread cold cake with frosting before serving.
lemon cream cheese frosting Beat butter, cream cheese and rind in small bowl with electric mixer until light and fluffy; gradually beat in icing sugar.

prep and cook time 1 hour 25 minutes
serves 12
nutritional count per serving 32.1g total fat (6.1g saturated fat); 2416kJ (578 cal); 64.2g carbohydrate; 7g protein; 2.7g fibre

Economical boiled fruit cake

2¾ cups (500g) mixed dried fruit
1 cup (220g) firmly packed brown sugar
125g butter, chopped
½ cup (125ml) water
1 teaspoon mixed spice
½ teaspoon bicarbonate of soda
½ cup (125ml) sweet sherry
1 egg
1 cup (150g) plain flour
1 cup (150g) self-raising flour
⅓ cup (55g) blanched almonds
2 tablespoons sweet sherry, extra

1   Stir fruit, sugar, butter, the water, spice and soda in large saucepan over low heat, without boiling, until sugar dissolves and butter melts; bring to the boil. Reduce heat; simmer, covered, 5 minutes. Remove from heat; stir in sherry. Cool to room temperature.
2   Preheat oven to 160°C/140°C fan-assisted. Grease deep 20cm-round cake tin; line base and side with two layers of baking parchment, extending paper 5cm above side.
3   Stir egg and sifted flours into fruit mixture. Spread mixture into tin; decorate with almonds.
4   Bake cake about 1½ hours. Brush top of hot cake with extra sherry. Cover cake with foil; cool in pan.

prep and cook time 1 hour 45 minutes (plus cooling)
serves 12
nutritional count per serving 12.2g total fat (6.1g saturated fat); 1718kJ (411 cal); 64.6g carbohydrate; 5g protein; 3.7g fibre

Featherlight sponge

4 eggs
¾ cup (165g) caster sugar
⅔ cup (150g) cornflour
¼ cup (30g) custard powder
1 teaspoon cream of tartar
½ teaspoon bicarbonate of soda
300ml whipping cream
1 teaspoon vanilla extract
¼ cup (80g) strawberry jam
250g strawberries, sliced thinly
icing
1 cup (160g) icing sugar
10g butter, softened
1½ tablespoons milk, approximately
pink food colouring

1   Preheat oven to 200°C/180°C fan-assisted. Grease and flour two deep 22cm-round cake tins; shake out any excess flour.
2   Beat eggs and sugar in small bowl with electric mixer about 7 minutes or until thick and creamy. Transfer mixture to large bowl.
3   Sift dry ingredients together twice onto sheet of baking parchment. Sift flour mixture a third time evenly over egg mixture. Using whisk or large metal spoon, quickly and lightly fold flour mixture through egg mixture until incorporated. Spread mixture evenly into tins.
4   Bake sponges about 20 minutes or until they spring back when touched lightly in the centre. Turn immediately, top-side up, onto wire racks to cool.
5   Meanwhile, make icing.
6   Beat cream and extract in small bowl with electric mixture until firm peaks form. Place one un-iced sponge on serving plate, spread with jam and whipped cream; top with sliced strawberries.
7   Spread warm icing over remaining sponge; place on top of strawberries. Stand about 15 minutes or until set.
icing   Sift icing sugar into medium heatproof bowl; stir in butter and enough milk to form a firm paste. Tint with a few drops of food colouring. Stir over simmering water until icing is a pouring consistency.

prep and cook time 40 minutes
serves 12
nutritional count per serving 11.9g total fat (11.2g saturated fat); 1275kJ (305 cal); 45.5g carbohydrate; 3.2g protein; 0.6g fibre

Iced cupcakes

125g butter, softened
1 teaspoon vanilla extract
⅔ cup (150g) caster sugar
3 eggs
1½ cups (225g) self-raising flour
¾ cup (60ml) milk
glacé icing
1½ cups (240g) icing sugar
1 teaspoon butter
2 tablespoons milk, approximately

1 Preheat oven to 180°C/160°C fan-assisted. Line two deep 12-hole bun tins with paper cases.
2 Beat butter, extract, sugar, eggs, flour and milk in medium bowl with electric mixer at low speed until just combined. Increase speed to medium; beat about 3 minutes or until mixture is smooth and paler in colour. Drop slightly rounded tablespoons of mixture into paper cases.
3 Bake about 20 minutes. Turn, top-side up, onto wire racks to cool.
4 Meanwhile, make glacé icing; top cakes with icing.
glacé icing Sift icing sugar into small heatproof bowl; stir in butter and enough milk to give a firm paste. Set bowl over small saucepan of simmering water; stir until icing is spreadable.

prep and cook time 40 minutes (plus cooling)
makes 24
nutritional count per cake 5.4g total fat (3.2g saturated fat); 627kJ (150 cal); 23.1g carbohydrate; 1.9g protein; 0.4g fibre

Variations

sugared berry cupcakes Spread the top of the cakes with vanilla butter cream (see recipe opposite). Brush some fresh berries sparingly with lightly beaten egg white; gently roll the wet fruit in caster sugar. Position on the cake.

malted chocolate cupcakes Spread the top of the cake with chocolate butter cream (sift 1 tablespoon cocoa powder with the icing sugar used in the butter cream recipe). Cut Maltesers™ in half with a sharp knife. Pile generously over the butter cream.

strawberry creamcakes Spread the top of the cake with butter cream. Remove the green top from strawberries, slice thinly and arrange on top of the cake to make a flower. Brush with warmed, strained strawberry jam.

daisy cupcakes Spread the top of the cake with butter cream. Cut pink marshmallows in half horizontally; squeeze the ends together to form petals. Decorate the cake with petals; position a Smartie™ in the centre of each daisy.

Vanilla butter cream

125g butter, softened
1 teaspoon vanilla extract
1½ cups (240g) icing sugar
2 tablespoons milk

1 Beat butter and extract in small bowl with electric mixer until as white as possible.

2 Gradually beat in half the sifted icing sugar, milk, then remaining icing sugar. Tint with food colouring, if desired.

Banana cake with passionfruit icing

125g butter, softened
¾ cup (165g) firmly packed brown sugar
2 eggs
1½ cups (225g) self-raising flour
½ teaspoon bicarbonate of soda
1 teaspoon mixed spice
1 cup mashed banana
½ cup (120g) soured cream
¼ cup (60ml) milk
passionfruit icing
1½ cups (240g) icing sugar
1 teaspoon soft butter
2 tablespoons passionfruit pulp, approximately

You need approximately 2 large overripe bananas (460g) for this recipe and 2 large passionfruit.

1 Preheat oven to 180°C/160°C fan-assisted. Grease 15cm x 25cm loaf tin; line base with baking parchment.
2 Beat butter and sugar in small bowl with electric mixer until light and fluffy; beat in eggs, one at a time. Transfer to large bowl; stir in sifted dry ingredients, banana, soured cream and milk. Spread mixture into tin.
3 Bake cake about 50 minutes. Stand in tin 5 minutes; turn, top-side up, onto wire rack to cool.
4 Meanwhile, make passionfruit icing. Spread cake with icing.
passionfruit icing Combine ingredients in medium bowl.

prep and cook time 1 hour 25 minutes (plus cooling)
serves 10
nutritional count per serving 17g total fat (10.7g saturated fat); 1768kJ (423 cal); 61.5g carbohydrate; 4.7g protein; 1.9g fibre

Date slice

1½ cups (225g) plain flour
1¼ cups (185g) self-raising flour
150g chilled butter, chopped
1 tablespoon honey
1 egg
⅓ cup (80ml) milk, approximately
2 teaspoons milk, extra
1 tablespoon white sugar
date filling
3½ cups (500g) dried pitted dates, chopped coarsely
¾ cup (180ml) water
2 tablespoons finely grated lemon rind
2 tablespoons lemon juice

1   Grease 20cm x 30cm baking tin; line base with baking parchment, extending paper 5cm over long sides.
2   Sift flours into large bowl; rub in butter until mixture is crumbly. Stir in combined honey and egg and enough milk to make a firm dough. Knead on floured surface until smooth. Cover; refrigerate 30 minutes.
3   Meanwhile, make date filling.
4   Preheat oven to 200°C/180°C fan-assisted.
5   Divide dough in half. Roll one half large enough to cover base of tin; press into tin, spread filling over dough. Roll remaining dough large enough to cover filling. Brush with extra milk; sprinkle with sugar. Bake about 20 minutes; cool in tin.
date filling   Cook ingredients in medium saucepan, stirring, about 10 minutes or until thick and smooth. Cool to room temperature.

prep and cook time 1 hour 25 minutes (plus refrigeration)
makes 24
nutritional count per piece 5.7g total fat (3.6g saturated fat); 757kJ (181 cal); 28.2g carbohydrate;

Cinnamon teacake

60g butter, softened
1 teaspoon vanilla extract
²⁄₃ cup (150g) caster sugar
1 egg
1 cup (150g) self-raising flour
¹⁄₃ cup (80ml) milk
10g butter, melted, extra
1 teaspoon ground cinnamon
1 tablespoon caster sugar, extra

1 Preheat oven to 180°C/160°C fan-assisted. Grease deep 20cm-round cake tin; line base with baking parchment.
2 Beat butter, extract, sugar and egg in small bowl with electric mixer until light and fluffy, this will take about 10 minutes. Stir in sifted flour and milk. Spread mixture into tin.
3 Bake cake about 30 minutes. Turn cake onto wire rack then turn top-side up; brush top with extra butter, sprinkle with combined cinnamon and extra sugar. Serve warm with butter, if desired.

prep and cook time 45 minutes
serves 10
nutritional count per serving 6.8g total fat (4.2g saturated fat); 769kJ (184 cal); 27.8g carbohydrate; 2.5g protein; 0.6g fibre

Triple choc brownies

125g butter, chopped
200g dark eating chocolate, chopped coarsely
½ cup (110g) caster sugar
2 eggs, beaten lightly
1¼ cups (185g) plain flour
150g white eating chocolate, chopped coarsely
100g milk eating chocolate, chopped coarsely

1 Preheat oven to 180°C/160°C fan-assisted. Grease deep 19cm-square cake tin; line base and sides with baking parchment.
2 Combine butter and dark chocolate in medium saucepan; stir over low heat until melted. Cool 10 minutes.
3 Stir in sugar and egg, then flour; stir in white and milk chocolates. Spread mixture into tin.
4 Bake about 35 minutes or until mixture is firm to touch. Cool in tin. If desired, sprinkle with sifted icing sugar before cutting.

prep and cook time 55 minutes (plus cooling time)
serves 12
nutritional count per piece 20.8g total fat (12.8g saturated fat); 1555kJ (372 cal); 42.8g carbohydrate; 5.3g protein; 0.9g fibre

WINTER
BY THE FIRE

Winter by the Fire

HEARTY SOUPS

traditional STEAK & KIDNEY PIE

WARMING STEW
with filling dumplings

Sticky puddings

STEAMING BOWLS OF SOUP,
FRAGRANT STEWS AND DELICIOUS
PIES AND PUDDINGS THAT WILL PUT
A ROSY GLOW IN YOUR CHEEKS

Minestrone

1 cup (200g) dried borlotti beans
1 tablespoon olive oil
1 medium brown onion (150g), chopped coarsely
1 clove garlic, crushed
¼ cup (70g) tomato paste
1.5 litres (6 cups) water
2 cups (500ml) vegetable stock
700g bottled tomato pasta sauce
1 trimmed celery stalk (100g), chopped finely
1 medium carrot (120g), chopped finely
1 medium courgette (120g), chopped finely
80g green beans, trimmed, chopped finely
¾ cup (135g) macaroni pasta
⅓ cup coarsely chopped fresh basil

1   Place borlotti beans in medium bowl, cover with water; stand overnight, drain. Rinse under cold water; drain.
2   Heat oil in large saucepan; cook onion and garlic, stirring, until onion softens. Add paste; cook, stirring, 2 minutes. Add borlotti beans, the water, stock and pasta sauce; bring to the boil. Reduce heat; simmer, uncovered, about 1 hour or until beans are tender.
3   Add celery to soup; simmer, uncovered, 10 minutes. Add carrot, courgette and green beans; simmer, uncovered, about 20 minutes or until carrot is tender. Add pasta; simmer until pasta is tender.
4   Serve bowls of soup sprinkled with basil.

prep and cook time 2 hours 30 minutes (plus standing)
serves 6
nutritional count per serving 5.5g total fat (1g saturated fat); 1095kJ (262 cal); 39.9g carbohydrate; 9.4g protein; 6.5g fibre

Scotch broth

1kg lamb neck chops
¾ cup (150g) pearl barley
2.25 litres (9 cups) water
1 large brown onion (200g), cut into 1cm pieces
2 medium carrots (240g), cut into 1cm pieces
1 medium leek (350g), sliced thinly
2 cups (160g) finely shredded savoy cabbage
½ cup (60g) frozen peas
2 tablespoons coarsely chopped fresh flat-leaf parsley

1 Place chops, barley and the water in large saucepan; bring to the boil. Reduce heat; simmer, covered, 1 hour, skimming fat from surface occasionally.
2 Add onion, carrot and leek to pan; simmer, covered, about 30 minutes or until vegetables are tender.
3 Remove chops from soup mixture; when cool enough to handle, remove meat, chop coarsely. Discard bones.
4 Return meat to soup with cabbage and peas; cook, uncovered, about 10 minutes or until cabbage is tender.
5 Just before serving, sprinkle with parsley.

prep and cook time 1 hour 30 minutes
serves 4
nutritional count per serving 24.4g total fat (10.7g saturated fat); 2274kJ (544 cal); 32.8g carbohydrate; 43.2g protein; 10.6g fibre

Chunky beef & vegetable soup

2 tablespoons olive oil
600g stewing steak, trimmed, cut into 2cm pieces
1 medium brown onion (150g), chopped coarsely
1 clove garlic, crushed
1.5 litres (6 cups) water
1 cup (250ml) beef stock
400g can diced tomatoes
2 trimmed celery stalks (200g), cut into 1cm pieces
1 medium carrot (120g), cut into 1cm pieces
2 small potatoes (240g), cut into 1cm pieces
310g can corn kernels, rinsed, drained
½ cup (60g) frozen peas

1 Heat half of the oil in large saucepan; cook beef, in batches, until browned.
2 Heat remaining oil in same pan; cook onion and garlic, stirring, until onion softens. Return beef to pan with the water, stock and undrained tomatoes; bring to the boil. Reduce heat; simmer, covered, 1½ hours.
3 Add celery, carrot and potato to soup; simmer, uncovered, about 20 minutes or until vegetables are tender.
4 Add corn and peas to soup; stir over heat until peas are tender.

prep and cook time 2 hours 20 minutes
serves 4
nutritional count per serving 17g total fat (4.3g saturated fat); 1768kJ (423 cal); 26.7g carbohydrate; 36.9g protein; 7.5g fibre

Steak & kidney pie

300g beef ox kidneys
1.5g beef braising steak, chopped coarsely
2 medium brown onions (300g), sliced thinly
1 cup (250ml) beef stock
1 tablespoon soy sauce
¼ cup (35g) plain flour
½ cup (125ml) water
2 sheets ready-rolled puff pastry
1 egg, beaten lightly

1 Remove fat from kidneys; chop kidneys finely. Place kidneys, steak, onion, stock and sauce in large saucepan; simmer, covered, about 1 hour or until steak is tender. Preheat oven to 200°C/180°C fan-assisted.
2 Stir blended flour and water into beef mixture; stir until mixture boils and thickens. Transfer to 1.5-litre (6-cup) ovenproof dish.
3 Cut pastry into 6cm rounds. Overlap rounds on beef mixture; brush with egg. Bake pies about 15 minutes or until browned.

prep and cook time 1 hour 50 minutes
serves 6
nutritional count per serving 25.8g total fat (12.2g saturated fat); 2546kJ (609 cal); 27.2g carbohydrate; 65.9g protein; 1.6g fibre

Curried sausages

800g thick beef sausages
20g butter
1 medium brown onion (150g), chopped coarsely
1 tablespoon curry powder
2 teaspoons plain flour
2 large carrots (360g), chopped coarsely
2 trimmed celery stalks (200g), chopped coarsely
500g baby new potatoes, halved
2 cups (500ml) beef stock
1 cup loosely packed fresh flat-leaf parsley leaves

1 Cook sausages, in batches, in heated deep large frying pan until cooked through. Cut each sausage into thirds.
2 Melt butter in same cleaned pan; cook onion, stirring, until soft. Add curry powder and flour; cook, stirring, 2 minutes.
3 Add vegetables and stock; bring to the boil. Reduce heat; simmer, covered, about 15 minutes or until vegetables are tender. Add sausages; simmer, uncovered, until sauce thickens slightly. Stir in parsley.

prep and cook time 55 minutes
serves 4
nutritional count per serving 55.8g total fat (27.3g saturated fat); 3177kJ (760 cal); 29.8g carbohydrate; 30.1g protein; 12.8g fibre

Beef stew with parsley dumplings

1kg stewing steak, cut into 5cm pieces
2 tablespoons plain flour
2 tablespoons olive oil
20g butter
2 medium brown onions (300g), chopped coarsely
2 cloves garlic, crushed
2 medium carrots (240g), chopped coarsely
1 cup (250ml) dry red wine
2 tablespoons tomato paste
2 cups (500ml) beef stock
4 sprigs fresh thyme
parsley dumplings
1 cup (150g) self-raising flour
50g butter
1 egg, beaten lightly
¼ cup (20g) coarsely grated parmesan cheese
¼ cup finely chopped fresh flat-leaf parsley
⅓ cup (50g) drained sun-dried tomatoes, chopped
¼ cup (60ml) milk

1 Preheat oven to 180°C/160°C fan-assisted.

2 Coat beef in flour; shake off excess. Heat oil in large flameproof dish; cook beef, in batches, until browned.

3 Melt butter in same dish; cook onion, garlic and carrot, stirring, until vegetables soften. Add wine; cook, stirring, until liquid reduces to ¼ cup. Return beef with paste, stock and thyme; bring to the boil. Cover; cook in oven 1¾ hours.

4 Meanwhile, make parsley dumpling mixture.

5 Remove dish from oven. Drop level tablespoons of dumpling mixture, about 2cm apart, onto top of stew. Cook, uncovered, about 20 minutes until dumplings are browned lightly and cooked through.

parsley dumplings Place flour in bowl; rub in butter. Stir in egg, cheese, parsley, tomato and enough milk to make a soft, sticky dough.

prep and cook time 2 hours 30 minutes
serves 4
nutritional count per serving 39.7g total fat (17.4g saturated fat); 3457kJ (827 cal); 43g carbohydrate; 63.9g protein; 6.7g fibre

Shepherd's pie

30g butter
1 medium brown onion (150g), chopped finely
1 medium carrot (120g), chopped finely
½ teaspoon dried mixed herbs
4 cups (750g) chopped cooked lamb
¼ cup (70g) tomato paste
¼ cup (60ml) tomato sauce
2 tablespoons worcestershire sauce
2 cups (500ml) beef stock
2 tablespoons plain flour
⅓ cup (80ml) water
potato topping
5 medium potatoes (1kg), chopped
60g butter, chopped
¼ cup (60ml) milk

1 Preheat oven to 200°C/180°C fan-assisted. Oil shallow 2.5-litre (10-cup) ovenproof dish.

2 Make potato topping.

3 Heat butter in large saucepan; cook onion and carrot, stirring, until tender. Add mixed herbs and lamb; cook, stirring, 2 minutes. Stir in paste, sauces and stock, then blended flour and water; stir over heat until mixture boils and thickens. Pour mixture into dish.

4 Place heaped tablespoons of potato topping on lamb mixture. Bake about 20 minutes or until browned lightly and heated through.

potato topping Boil, steam or microwave potatoes until tender; drain. Mash with butter and milk until smooth.

prep and cook time 1 hour
serves 4
nutritional count per serving 36.2g total fat (20.2g saturated fat); 2976kJ (712 cal); 44.7g carbohydrate; 48.8g protein; 6.6g fibre

Curried chicken pies

1.6kg chicken
90g butter
1 small leek (200g), chopped finely
1 medium white onion (150g), chopped finely
1 medium red pepper (200g), chopped finely
2 trimmed celery stalks (200g), chopped finely
3 teaspoons curry powder
¼ teaspoon chilli powder
¼ cup (35g) plain flour
⅓ cup (80g) soured cream
½ cup finely chopped fresh flat-leaf parsley
2 sheets ready-rolled puff pastry
1 egg, beaten lightly

1   Place chicken in large saucepan, add enough water to just cover chicken; bring to the boil. Reduce heat; simmer, uncovered, 1 hour. Remove pan from heat; when cool enough to handle, remove chicken from stock. Reserve 1¾ cups (430ml) of the stock for this recipe.
2   Preheat oven to 200°C/180°C fan-assisted.
3   Remove skin and bones from chicken; chop chicken flesh roughly.
4   Heat butter in large frying pan, add leek, onion, capsicum and celery; cook, stirring, until vegetables are soft.
5   Add curry powder and chilli powder; cook, stirring, until fragrant. Stir in flour. Add reserved stock, stir over heat until mixture boils and thickens; reduce heat, simmer 1 minute, remove from heat. Stir in sour cream, chicken and parsley. Spoon mixture into six 1¼-cup (310ml) ovenproof dishes.
6   Cut pastry into six rounds large enough to cover top of each dish. Lightly brush pastry with egg. Place pies on oven tray.
7   Bake pies 10 minutes. Reduce oven to 180°C/160°C fan-assisted; bake further 15 minutes or until pastry is golden brown.

prep and cook time 2 hours 30 minutes (plus standing)
serves 6
nutritional count per serving 52.8g total fat (25.4g saturated fat); 3001kJ (718 cal); 28.5g carbohydrate; 33.3g protein; 3g fibre

THE BEAUTY OF THESE INDIVIDUAL PIES IS
THAT YOU CAN FREEZE THEM AND HAVE THEM
AT THE READY FOR THE NEXT TIME YOU NEED
A WARM-YOU-UP DINNER FOR ONE OR MORE.

Sticky date pudding & butterscotch sauce

1¼ cups (200g) pitted dried dates
1¼ cups (310ml) boiling water
1 teaspoon bicarbonate of soda
50g butter, chopped
½ cup (100g) firmly packed brown sugar
2 eggs, beaten lightly
1 cup (150g) self-raising flour
butterscotch sauce
¾ cup (150g) firmly packed brown sugar
300ml double cream
80g butter

1 Preheat oven to 180°C/160°C fan-assisted. Grease deep 20cm-round cake tin; line base and sides with baking parchment.
2 Combine dates and the water in medium heatproof bowl. Stir in soda; stand 5 minutes.
3 Blend or process date mixture with butter and sugar until pureed. Add eggs and flour; blend or process until just combined. Pour mixture into tin.
4 Bake about 1 hour. Stand in tin 10 minutes; turn onto serving plate
5 Meanwhile, make butterscotch sauce.
6 Serve pudding warm with butterscotch sauce.
butterscotch sauce Stir ingredients in medium saucepan over low heat until smooth.

prep and cook time 1 hour 10 minutes (plus standing)
serves 6
nutritional count per serving 41.5g total fat (26.6g saturated fat); 3068kJ (734 cal); 82g carbohydrate; 6.5g protein; 4.2g fibre

Chocolate self-saucing pudding

60g butter
½ cup (125ml) milk
½ teaspoon vanilla extract
¾ cup (165g) caster sugar
1 cup (150g) self-raising flour
1 tablespoon cocoa powder
¾ cup (165g) firmly packed brown sugar
1 tablespoon cocoa powder, extra
2 cups (500ml) boiling water

1 Preheat oven to 180°C/160°C fan-assisted. Grease 1.5-litre (6-cup) ovenproof dish.
2 Melt butter with milk in medium saucepan. Remove from heat; stir in extract and caster sugar then sifted flour and cocoa. Spread into dish.
3 Sift brown sugar and extra cocoa over mixture; gently pour boiling water over mixture.
4 Bake pudding about 40 minutes or until centre is firm. Stand 5 minutes before serving.

prep and cook time 1 hour
serves 6
nutritional count per serving 9.7g total fat (6.2g saturated fat); 1676kJ (401 cal); 73.4g carbohydrate; 3.8g protein; 1.1g fibre

College pudding

⅓ cup (110g) raspberry jam
1 egg
½ cup (110g) caster sugar
1 cup (150g) self-raising flour
½ cup (125ml) milk
25g butter, melted
1 tablespoon boiling water
1 teaspoon vanilla extract

1   Grease four 1-cup (250ml) metal moulds; divide jam among moulds.
2   Beat egg and sugar in small bowl with electric mixer until thick and creamy. Fold in sifted flour and milk, in two batches; fold in combined butter, the water and extract.
3   Spoon pudding mixture over jam. Cover each mould with pleated baking parchment and foil (to allow puddings to expand as they cook); secure with kitchen string.
4   Place puddings in large saucepan with enough boiling water to come halfway up sides of moulds. Cover pan with tight-fitting lid; boil 25 minutes, replenishing water as necessary to maintain level. Stand in moulds 5 minutes; turn onto serving plates. Serve puddings with cream, if desired.

prep and cook time 35 minutes
serves 4
nutritional count per serving 8.1g total fat (4.7g saturated fat); 1676kJ (401 cal); 73.7g carbohydrate; 6.5g protein; 1.7g fibre

Golden syrup dumplings

1¼ cups (185g) self-raising flour
30g butter
⅓ cup (115g) golden syrup
⅓ cup (80ml) milk
sauce
30g butter
¾ cup (165g) firmly packed brown sugar
½ cup (175g) golden syrup
1⅔ cups (410ml) water

1 Sift flour into medium bowl; rub in butter. Gradually stir in golden syrup and milk.
2 Make sauce.
3 Drop rounded tablespoonfuls of mixture into simmering sauce; simmer, covered, about 20 minutes. Serve dumplings with sauce.
sauce Stir ingredients in medium saucepan over heat, without boiling, until sugar dissolves. Bring to the boil, without stirring. Reduce heat; simmer, uncovered, 5 minutes.

prep and cook time 30 minutes
serves 4
nutritional count per serving 13.6g total fat (8.7g saturated fat); 2788kJ (667 cal); 128g carbohydrate; 5.6g protein; 1.8g fibre

THESE DUMPLINGS ARE MADE FROM A SCONE-TYPE DOUGH. COOKING THEM IN THE SAUCE INFUSES THEM WITH THE SWEET FLAVOUR. YOU'LL NEED TO USE A SAUCEPAN LARGE ENOUGH TO ALLOW THE DUMPLINGS TO EXPAND IN THE SIMMERING SAUCE.

Bread & butter pud

6 slices white bread (270g)
40g butter, softened
½ cup (80g) sultanas
¼ teaspoon ground nutmeg
custard
1½ cups (375ml) milk
2 cups (500ml) double cream
⅓ cup (75g) caster sugar
½ teaspoon vanilla extract
4 eggs

1 Preheat oven to 160°C/140°C fan-assisted. Grease shallow 2-litre (8-cup) ovenproof dish. Make custard.
2 Trim crusts from bread. Spread each slice with butter; cut into four triangles. Layer bread, overlapping, in dish; sprinkle with sultanas. Pour custard over bread; sprinkle with nutmeg.
3 Place dish in large baking dish; add enough boiling water to come halfway up sides of dish. Bake pudding about 45 minutes or until set. Remove pudding from baking dish; stand 5 minutes before serving.
custard Bring milk, cream, sugar and extract in medium saucepan to the boil. Whisk eggs in large bowl; whisking constantly, gradually add hot milk mixture to egg mixture.

prep and cook time 1 hour 10 minutes
serves 6
nutritional count per serving 48.6g total fat (30.4g saturated fat); 2859kJ (684 cal); 49.3g carbohydrate; 12.4g protein; 1.8g fibre

Baked custard

6 eggs
1 teaspoon vanilla extract
⅓ cup (75g) caster sugar
1 litre (4 cups) hot milk
¼ teaspoon ground nutmeg

1 Preheat oven to 160°C/140°C fan-assisted. Grease shallow 1.5-litre (6-cup) ovenproof dish.
2 Whisk eggs, extract and sugar in large bowl; gradually whisk in hot milk. Pour custard mixture into dish; sprinkle with nutmeg.
3 Place dish in larger baking dish; add enough boiling water to baking dish to come halfway up sides of dish.
4 Bake custard, uncovered, about 45 minutes. Remove custard from baking dish; stand 5 minutes before serving.

prep and cook time 50 minutes
serves 6
nutritional count per serving 11.8g total fat (5.9g saturated fat); 995kJ (238 cal); 20.7g carbohydrate; 12.3g protein; 0g fibre

Glossary

ALLSPICE also known as pimento or Jamaican pepper; available whole or ground.

ALMONDS
blanched skins removed.
flaked paper-thin slices.
ground also known as almond meal; nuts are powdered to a coarse flour texture.
slivered cut lengthways.

BASIL An aromatic herb; there are many types, but the most commonly used is sweet basil.

BAY LEAVES Aromatic leaves from the bay tree available fresh or dried; used to add a strong, slightly peppery flavour to soups, stocks and casseroles.

BICARBONATE OF SODA also called baking soda.

BORLOTTI BEANS also known as roman beans, they can be eaten fresh or dried. Are a pale pink or beige colour with darker red spots.

BRAN, UNPROCESSED is the coarse outer husk of cereal grains, and can be found in health food stores and supermarkets.

BUTTERMILK fresh low-fat milk cultured to give a slightly sour, tangy taste; low-fat yogurt or milk can be substituted.

BUTTERNUT SQUASH sometimes used interchangeably with the word pumpkin, butternut squash is a member of the gourd family. Various types can be substituted for one another.

CAPERS the grey-green buds of a warm climate shrub sold either dried and salted or pickled in vinegar brine.

CHEESE
brie soft-ripened cow-milk cheese with a delicate, creamy texture and a rich, sweet taste. Best served at room temperature, brie should have a bloomy white rind and creamy, voluptuous centre which becomes runny with ripening.
cheddar the most common cow's milk cheese; should be aged and hard.
cottage fresh, white, unripened curd cheese with a lumpy consistency and mild flavour.
parmesan a sharp-tasting, dry, hard cheese, made from skimmed or semi-skimmed milk and aged for at least a year.
ricotta a soft, sweet, moist, white, cow-milk cheese with a low fat content (about 8.5 per cent) and a slightly grainy texture. The name roughly translates as 'cooked again' and refers to ricotta's manufacture from a whey that is itself a by-product of other cheese making.

CHERVIL also known as cicily; mildly fennel-flavoured herb with curly dark-green leaves.

CHILLI POWDER the Asian variety is the hottest, made from ground chillies; it can be used as a substitute for fresh chillies in the proportion of ½ teaspoon ground chilli powder to 1 medium chopped fresh chilli.

CHIVES related to the onion and leek, with subtle onion flavour.

CHOCOLATE HAZELNUT SPREAD we use Nutella. It was originally developed when chocolate was hard to source during World War II; hazelnuts were added to extend the chocolate supply.

CINNAMON dried inner bark of the shoots of the cinnamon tree. Available as a stick or ground.

COCOA POWDER also known as unsweetened cocoa; cocoa beans that have been fermented, roasted, shelled, ground into powder then cleared of most of the fat content.

COCONUT
desiccated unsweetened and concentrated, dried finely shredded.
flaked dried flaked coconut flesh.
shredded thin strips of dried coconut.

CORN KERNELS sometimes known as niblets; available canned and frozen.

CORNFLOUR also known as cornstarch; used as a thickening agent in cooking.

CREAM OF TARTAR the acid ingredient in baking powder; added to confectionery mixtures to help prevent sugar from crystallising. Keeps frostings creamy and improves volume when beating egg whites.

CREAM, SOURED a thick commercially-cultured soured cream. Minimum fat content 35%.

CURRY POWDER a blend of ground spices; choose mild or hot to suit your taste and the recipe.

DATE fruit of the date palm tree, eaten fresh or dried, on their own or in prepared dishes. About 4cm to 6cm in length, oval and plump, thin-skinned, with a honey-sweet flavour and sticky texture.

DILL also known as dill weed; used fresh or dried, in seed form or ground; has a sweet anise/celery flavour with distinctive feathery, frond-like fresh leaves.

FIGS small, soft, pear-shaped fruit with a sweet pulpy flesh full of tiny edible seeds. Figs may also be glacéd (candied), dried or canned in sugar syrup.

FLAT-LEAF PARSLEY also known as continental parsley or italian parsley.

FLOUR
plain all-purpose flour.
rice extremely fine flour made from ground rice.
self-raising plain flour sifted with baking powder (a raising agent consisting mainly of 2 parts cream of

tartar to 1 part bicarbonate of soda) in the proportion of 150g flour to 2 level teaspoons baking powder.

GINGER also known as green or root ginger; the thick gnarled root of a tropical plant.

GOLDEN SYRUP a by-product of refined sugarcane; pure maple syrup or honey can be substituted.

HERBS we have specified when to use fresh or dried herbs. Use dried (not ground) herbs in the proportions of 1:4 for fresh herbs, for example 1 teaspoon dried herbs instead of 4 teaspoons (1 tablespoon) chopped fresh herbs.

JUNIPER BERRIES these have a bittersweet taste. Used widely in Northern Europe and Scandinavia in marinades, roast pork, and sauerkraut.

MANGETOUT ('eat all') also known as snow peas.

MIXED SPICE a blend of ground spices usually consisting of cinnamon, allspice and nutmeg.

MUESLI also known as granola; a combination of grains (mainly oats), nuts and dried fruits.

MUSTARD
dijon a pale brown, distinctively flavoured fairly mild French mustard.
wholegrain also known as seeded. A French-style coarse-grain mustard made from crushed mustard seeds and dijon-style French mustard.

NUTMEG dried nut of an evergreen tree; available in ground form or you can grate your own with a fine grater.

OIL
olive mono-unsaturated; made from the pressing of tree-ripened olives. Extra virgin and virgin are the best, obtained from the first pressings of the olive, while extra light or light refers to the taste, not fat levels.
vegetable Any number of oils sourced from plants rather than animal fats.

PAPRIKA ground, dried red bell pepper (capsicum); available sweet, smoked or hot.

PASSIONFRUIT also known as granadilla; a small tropical fruit, native to Brazil, comprised of a tough dark-purple skin surrounding edible black sweet-sour seeds.

PEARL BARLEY the husk is removed, then hulled and polished so that the 'pearl' of the original grain remains, much the same as white rice.

PEPITAS pale green kernels of dried pumpkin seeds; they can be bought plain or salted.

PEPPERCORNS available in black, white, red or green.

PISTACHIOS pale green, delicately flavoured nut inside hard off-white shells. To peel, soak shelled nuts in boiling water about 5 minutes; drain, then pat dry.

POLENTA a flour-like cereal made of ground corn (maize); similar to cornmeal but finer and lighter in colour; also the name of the dish made from it.

PROSCIUTTO salted-cured, air-dried (unsmoked), pressed ham; usually sold in paper-thin slices, ready to eat.

PUMPKIN Also known as squash; is a member of the gourd family and used as an ingredient or eaten on its own. Various types can be substituted for one another.

ROLLED GRAINS includes rice, barley, oats, rye and triticale; the whole grain has been steamed and flattened – not the quick-cook variety. Available from health food stores and supermarkets.

rolled oats traditional Whole oat grains that have been steamed and flattened. Not the quick-cook variety.

ROSEWATER extract made from crushed rose petals; available from health food stores and speciality grocers.

SHERRY, SWEET fortified wine consumed as an aperitif or used in cooking.

SOY SAUCE made from fermented soy beans; several variations are available.

SUGAR We used coarse, granulated table sugar, unless otherwise specified.
brown an extremely soft, fine granulated sugar retaining molasses for its deep colour and flavour.
caster also known as superfine or finely granulated table sugar.
icing also known as confectioners' sugar or powdered sugar.

SWEET POTATO fleshy root vegetable; available with red or white flesh.

THYME a member of the mint family; has tiny grey-green leaves that give off a pungent minty, light-lemon aroma. Dried thyme comes in both leaf and powdered form.

TOMATO
cherry also known as tiny tim or tom thumb tomatoes; small and round.
tomato paste triple-concentrated
purée used to flavour soups, stews, sauces and casseroles.
sun-dried available loose (by weight) or in packets (not packed in oil).

VANILLA EXTRACT obtained from vanilla beans infused in water; a non-alcoholic version of essence.

VINEGAR
cider made from fermented apples.
brown malt made from fermented malt and beech shavings.
white made from spirit of cane sugar.

WORCESTERSHIRE SAUCE a thin, dark-brown, spicy sauce used as seasoning for meat and gravies, and as a condiment.

YOGURT an unflavoured, full-fat cows' milk yogurt has been used in these recipes unless stated otherwise.

Index

Conversion charts

measures

The cup and spoon measurements used in this book are metric: one measuring cup holds approximately 250ml; one metric tablespoon holds 20ml; one metric teaspoon holds 5ml.

All cup and spoon measurements are level. The most accurate way of measuring dry ingredients is to weigh them. When measuring liquids, use a clear glass or plastic jug with the metric markings.

We use large eggs with an average weight of 60g. This book contains recipes for dishes made with raw or lightly cooked eggs. These should be avoided by vulnerable people such as pregnant and nursing mothers, invalids, the elderly, babies and young children.

dry measures

METRIC	IMPERIAL
15g	½oz
30g	1oz
60g	2oz
90g	3oz
125g	4oz (¼lb)
155g	5oz
185g	6oz
220g	7oz
250g	8oz (½lb)
280g	9oz
315g	10oz
345g	11oz
375g	12oz (¾lb)
410g	13oz
440g	14oz
470g	15oz
500g	16oz (1lb)
750g	24oz (1½lb)
1kg	32oz (2lb)

liquid measures

METRIC	IMPERIAL
30ml	1 fluid oz
60ml	2 fluid oz
100ml	3 fluid oz
125ml	4 fluid oz
150ml	5 fluid oz (¼ pint/1 gill)
190ml	6 fluid oz
250ml	8 fluid oz
300ml	10 fluid oz (½ pint)
500ml	16 fluid oz
600ml	20 fluid oz (1 pint)
1000ml (1 litre)	1¾ pints

length measures

METRIC	IMPERIAL
3mm	⅛in
6mm	¼in
1cm	½in
2cm	¾in
2.5cm	1in
5cm	2in
6cm	2½in
8cm	3in
10cm	4in
13cm	5in
15cm	6in
18cm	7in
20cm	8in
23cm	9in
25cm	10in
28cm	11in
30cm	12in (1ft)

oven temperatures

These oven temperatures are only a guide for conventional ovens. For fan-assisted ovens, check the manufacturer's manual.

	°C (CELSIUS)	°F (FAHRENHEIT)	GAS MARK
Very low	120	250	½
Low	150	275-300	1-2
Moderately low	160	325	3
Moderate	180	350-375	4-5
Moderately hot	200	400	6
Hot	220	425-450	7-8
Very hot	240	475	9

ACP Books are published by ACP Magazines a division of PBL Media Pty Limited

Published by ACP Books, a division of ACP Magazines Ltd, 54 Park St, Sydney; GPO Box 4088, Sydney, NSW 2001. telephone (02) 9282 8618; fax (02) 9267 9438. acpbooks@acpmagazines.com.au; www.acpbooks.com.au

Printed and bound in China

United Kingdom Distributed by Australian Consolidated Press (UK), phone (01604) 642 200; fax (01604) 642 300; books@acpuk.com

A catalogue record for this book is available from the British Library

ISBN 978-1-903777-83-1

© ACP Magazines Ltd 2010
ABN 18 053 273 546

Scanpan cookware is used in the AWW Test Kitchen.

To order books:
telephone: 01604 642 200
order online: www.acpuk.com